PRESENTED TO:

_____

FROM:

_____

DATE:

_____

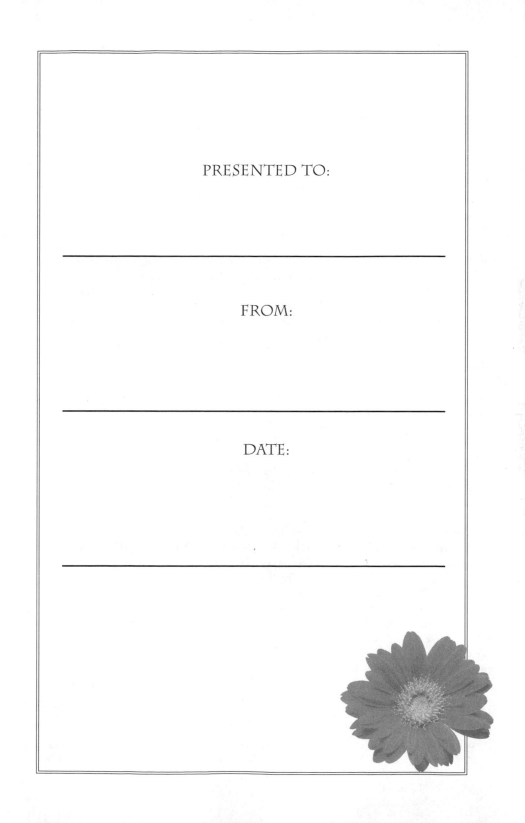

Honor® is an imprint of Cook Communications Ministries
Colorado Springs, Colorado 80918
Cook Communications, Paris, Ontario
Kingsway Communications, Eastbourne, England

MOTHERS OF INFLUENCE—INSPIRING STORIES OF WOMEN WHO MADE
A DIFFERENCE IN THEIR CHILDREN AND THEIR WORLD
© 2005 by BORDON BOOKS

First printing, 2005
Printed in the United States of America
3 4 5 6 7 Printing / Year 09 08 07 06 05

Developed by Bordon Books
Manuscript written and compiled by Heartland Editorial Management in association with
Snapdragon Group, Inc.
Cover Photo: comstock.com

ISBN: 1-56292-368-4

Para

Jessie Pacheco

de

Enrique-Araceli y Pacheco

MOTHERS *of* INFLUENCE

**INSPIRING STORIES OF WOMEN WHO MADE A DIFFERENCE
IN THEIR CHILDREN AND THEIR WORLD**

HONOR **HB** BOOKS

Inspiration and Motivation for the Seasons of Life

COOK COMMUNICATIONS MINISTRIES
Colorado Springs, Colorado • Paris, Ontario
KINGSWAY COMMUNICATIONS LTD
Eastbourne, England

"The woman who creates and sustains a home and

under whose hands children grow up to be strong and pure men and

women is a creator second only to God."

-Helen Maria Fiske Hunt Jackson

MOTHERS *of* INFLUENCE

TABLE OF CONTENTS

MOTHERS OF THE BIBLE

PRAYERS FOR YOUR CHILDREN

INTRODUCTION

Our mothers are our first teachers. They teach us to eat with a spoon, wash our hands after play, and share our toys. But first and foremost, our mothers are the keepers of the flame of our faith, teaching us to know and love and serve God. Their influence on our lives is too valuable to calculate. And the ripples of that influence through the generations are inestimable.

The mothers included in this book—*Mothers of Influence*—are women who have changed their worlds, most often through the accomplishments of their well-known offspring. Each courageous mother has made a major contribution both inside and outside the walls of her home. Each exemplifies a child-rearing principle that we feel will be of great value to you as you raise your own children.

We hope that reading about these remarkable women will inspire you and learning their child-rearing principles will allow you to guide your own children as they strive to reach their full, God-given potential. Then you will also be—a mother of influence.

MOTHER

You painted no Madonnas
On chapel walls in Rome,
But with a touch diviner
You lived one in your home.

You wrote no lofty poems
That critics counted art,
But with a nobler vision
You lived them in your heart.

You carved no shapeless marble
To some high soul design,
But with a finer sculpture
You shaped this soul of mine.

You built no great cathedrals
That centuries applaud,
But with a grace exquisite
Your life cathedraled God.

Had I the gift of Raphael
Or Michelangelo,
Oh, what a rare Madonna
My mother's life would show.

THOMAS W. FESSENDEN

ANGELENA RICE

1924-1985

CONDOLEEZA RICE'S mother, Angelena, passed on a love of music,

a legacy of higher education, a sense of self-worth, and a bold religious

faith to her daughter, who would one day serve as National Security

Advisor to President George W. Bush.

⚬❈⚬

The tall, beautiful black woman and her young daughter carefully perused the colorful children's dresses on the rack before selecting an outfit for the seven-year-old to try on. They headed for the fitting room, but a white saleswoman blocked their way. It was 1961 in Birmingham, Alabama, and racial segregation was the law of the South.

"This is reserved for white customers only," the salesclerk said and then directed Angelena Rice and Condi to a storage room reserved for "colored" people. It did not sit well with Angelena, who knew her position in Christ. She was a teacher of music and science at an all-black high school and much better educated than the woman standing in her way. In no uncertain terms, Angelena informed the clerk that her daughter would change in that dressing room, or she would take her money to another department store.

The clerk hesitated. It was possible she could lose her job, but it was certain that she would lose her sales commission if the mother and daughter walked out of the store. Condoleeza still remembers how nervous and apprehensive the clerk was when she guided Condi and her mother into a remote whites-only dressing room and stood guarding the door, afraid someone would find out she had let them in.

Another time when a salesclerk scolded young Condi for touching a hat, Angelena told her daughter to touch every hat in the store. Condoleeza did—happily. Angelena was that determined racism would never chart her daughter's future.

Since the time of slavery, Condoleeza Rice's family had used education and their faith in God as the way to overcome racial prejudice. Condi learned to read as a toddler, and by the age of three, she was learning to play the piano, as well as taking French and figure skating lessons. John, her father, pastored Westminster Presbyterian Church in Birmingham and became dean of Stillman College, where her grandfather had graduated. Later, he would serve as vice chancellor of the University of Denver.

Condi, who graduated from high school at the age of fifteen, was the third generation of the Rice family to go to college. At the University of Denver, she began as a music major. But Condi soon realized she would never be good enough to compete on the world stage and cast around for another major. Soon she found her niche—she was simply mesmerized with international studies. At the age of nineteen, she received her bachelor's degree and went on to earn a doctorate.

> WE REJOICE IN THE HOPE OF THE GLORY OF GOD. NOT ONLY SO, BUT WE ALSO REJOICE IN OUR SUF-FERINGS, BECAUSE WE KNOW THAT SUFFER-ING PRODUCES PER-SEVERANCE; PERSE-VERANCE, CHARAC-TER; AND CHARACTER, HOPE. AND HOPE DOES NOT DISAP-POINT US, BECAUSE GOD HAS POURED OUT HIS LOVE INTO OUR HEARTS BY THE HOLY SPIRIT, WHOM HE HAS GIVEN US.
>
> ROMANS 5:2-5 NIV

By the time she was twenty-six, Condoleeza was an assistant professor at Stanford University, but that wasn't enough to satisfy this ambitious young woman. Twelve years later, she became the first female, non-white, and youngest person ever to serve as Stanford's provost. Condi crowned her long list of "firsts" by joining the Bush campaign and becoming the country's first woman to serve as National Security Advisor. Her stunning success was no doubt due, at least in part, to her mother, who taught her that she was a child of God and could do anything with His help.

A Mother of Influence teaches her children who they are in Christ.

ELIZABETH ANNE EVEREST

Unknown -1895

WINSTON CHURCHILL'S nanny, Elizabeth, lived to instill

godliness and biblical truth into the life of an unhappy boy.

⌘

A s a child, his own parents and other adults often referred to
Winston Churchill as a monster. He was incorrigible—kicking,
screaming, hiding, bullying. One day, he stood defiantly before
his Christian nanny, Mrs. Elizabeth Anne Everest, and told her that
before he would do his mathematics lesson, he would "bow down and
worship graven images."

Such blasphemy! His bluff worked for a while, but Mrs. Everest was
too wise for such shenanigans and knew his unruly behavior masked a
hurting child, who desperately longed for love and nurturing.

Winston was born two months prematurely on November 30, 1874, to
upper-class Lord and Lady Randolph Churchill at Blenheim Palace during the Victorian era when children were typically turned over to a wet
nurse after birth. It is unlikely that he ever really bonded with his mother,
who largely ignored him.

However, God had another plan to bring comfort to this special child.
A few months after Winston's birth, Mrs. Everest (whom Winston would
call "Woom"—short for "Woomany") was hired as his nanny on a cold
blustery day in February of 1875.

Churchill, who became the most famous and celebrated British
author, orator, and politician of the twentieth century, wrote in My Early
Life (his autobiography), "I loved my mother dearly—but at a distance.
My nanny was my confidante. Mrs. Everest it was who looked after me

and tended all my wants. It was to her I poured out all my troubles."

His nanny was his disciplinarian, as well as the one who doctored his banged-up knees and cradled his head when he was sick. She was the one who told him Bible stories and taught him to pray. Being a nanny was not simply an occupation for Mrs. Everett, it was a calling from God, which she took seriously.

Serving not only as surrogate mother, Mrs. Everest was also the one person who taught Winston the principles of the Christian faith, which he would eventually embrace, rallying his nation and interceding for Britain while at war with the Nazis. He believed the Nazis threatened Christian civilization with its "barbarous paganism" and that every Christian's duty was "to preserve the structure of humane, enlightened, Christian society." All this he had learned from his nanny, who had invested her life in that of a troubled child.

As a boy, Winston eagerly memorized his favorite passages from the Bible. He and "Woom" sang hymns of the church, spoke of the heroes of the faith, and imagined aloud what Jesus might look like, or how Heaven would be. Woom explained the world to him in Christian terms. As a devoted intercessor, Mrs. Everest most likely prayed over her sleeping charge, asking her Heavenly Father to fulfill the powerful purpose she sensed on his life.

But like many young men of this age, when he reached early adulthood, Winston immersed himself in the anti-Christian rationalism that had swept the globe. It was not until he traveled as a journalist to South Africa during the Boer War and was captured that he returned to the faith he had learned at his nanny's knee. In a daring attempt, Winston finally escaped the stench of his South African prison and hopped a train heading into Portuguese East Africa, making him a hero in Britain. From that moment on, his faith defined him.

Violet Asquith once wrote of Churchill that in his "solitary childhood and unhappy school days, Mrs. Everest was his comforter, his strength and stay, his one source of unfailing human understanding. She was the fireside at which he dried his tears and warmed his heart. She was the night-light by his bed. She was his security."

When Winston Churchill addressed the world over the radio airwaves

> [THE LORD SAID,] "ASK OF ME, AND I WILL GIVE YOU THE NATIONS FOR YOUR INHERITANCE, AND THE ENDS OF THE EARTH FOR YOUR POSSESSION."
>
> PSALM 2:8 NKJV

during the dark days of World War II, he also was the voice of security to people everywhere—the light of Christ shining in a world threatened by unspeakable evil. Because of Mrs. Everest, when it was time to lead the world, Churchill stood ready with a strong, unyielding faith.

Her influence on him undoubtedly affected the future of every person in the Western world, because it was her words and the Scriptures she had read to him that rang in his ears as he stood against Hitler's evil. Thus, Elizabeth Everest was a Mother of Influence even though she had no children of her own.

Behind this great man of vision and fortitude, lay the simple teachings of a devoted nanny who fulfilled her God-ordained mission by pouring herself into the life and destiny of a little boy. She is a model for the many women who mother children who are not their own.

A Mother of Influence shares her passion for God with all children.

SUSAN KOERNER WRIGHT

1831-1889

WILBUR AND ORVILLE WRIGHT. Susan Wright supported her children in their childhood and adult ventures, which led them to become the world's first pioneers of sustained, powered flight.

In today's world, Susan Wright might have been a computer engineer or a designer of new toys, appliances, or SUVs. Even in the nineteenth century she was unusual, a woman with mechanical aptitude who spent hours—winter and summer—in the shop of her carriage-maker father on their Indiana farm. Put a hammer into Susan's hand, and she knew which end to hit the nail with. She understood tools, how they worked, and what would make them more useful. It was only natural that one day her sons Orville and Wilbur Wright would inherit some of her skills.

Susan and her husband, Milton, whom she met at Hartsville College in Indiana, were the perfect match. Both wanted to serve the United Brethren Church, and both encouraged their children to read and learn. Bishop Milton Wright was the theologian and philosopher, who would be hard-pressed to identify a hammer, much less use one. Susan was the mechanical one, the one who often made toys for her children and household appliances for herself. After all, she had been the top student in her mathematics class in college, and she had studied science as well as literature.

Susan and Milton, who had seven children (two died in infancy), shared a love of learning for the sake of learning. Their home had two libraries—one full of books on theology and another full of volumes on a variety of topics ranging from Shakespeare to ornithology. It was a lov-

DO YOU SEE A MAN
SKILLED IN HIS
WORK? HE WILL
STAND BEFORE
KINGS; HE WILL
NOT STAND BEFORE
OBSCURE MEN.

PROVERBS 22:29 NASB

ing, protective home, and the Wright brothers thrived in it.

"We were lucky enough to grow up in an environment where there was always encouragement to children to pursue intellectual interests," Orville Wright once said, "to investigate whatever aroused curiosity. In a different kind of environment, our curiosity might have been nipped long before it could have borne fruit."

No one in the Wright home ever clipped the Wright brothers' wings. Their father once brought them a toy helicopter, and their minds took flight. But it was their mother who nurtured their mechanical abilities and helped turn their dreams of flight into reality. When Orville and Wilbur needed practical mechanical advice and inspiration, she was the one they went to.

Not that Susan raised two perfect boys. Orville and Wilbur fought and squabbled like most brothers, but Wilbur once wrote, "From the time we were little children, my brother Orville and myself lived together, played together, worked together, and, in fact, thought together. We usually owned all of our toys in common, talked over our thoughts and aspirations so that nearly everything that was done in our lives has been the result of conversations, suggestions, and discussions between us." And their mother, Susan.

Wilbur was the scholar and athlete; the younger Orville, known as the mischief maker, was more interested in printing. He also liked to take things apart and put them back together. They would one day own a bicycle shop together.

When Wilbur was hit in the face during an ice-hockey game, it appeared to be a minor injury. But he developed heart palpitations and later experienced depression from being homebound. His mother had already developed tuberculosis, so despite Wilbur's desire to attend Yale, he decided to stay home and take care of Susan. As she had been there for him as a child, so he was there for her in her illness.

Susan died of tuberculosis on July 4, 1889, in Dayton, Ohio, never to experience the thrill of watching her sons' pioneering achievement of the first powered flight on December 17, 1903, at Kitty Hawk. Without their mother's help and encouragement throughout their childhood, the Wright brothers may never have taken wing on that gusty, frigid morning on the Outer Banks of North Carolina.

A Mother of Influence inspires a love of learning.

MAUD ARIEL
McKOY POWELL

Unknown - 1984

COLIN POWELL. Arie Powell taught her son Colin, the first

African-American Secretary of State under the administration

of President George W. Bush, to accept responsibility and to

always do the right thing.

⚜

"**A**lways do the right thing," Secretary of State Colin Powell once told a group of Wake Forest University graduates. "Do the right thing by setting your own internal standards of excellence, your own internal standards of behavior, and making sure that you meet them and exceed them. Do the right thing, even when you get no credit for it, even if you get hurt by doing the right thing. Do the right thing when no one is watching or will ever know about it. You will always know."

As a boy, Colin knew that if he didn't do the right thing, there would be consequences. His parents, Maud Ariel ("Arie") McKoy and Luther Theophilus Powell, immigrated separately to the United States in the 1920s looking for a brighter economic future. Both were people of faith, who had grown up in the Anglican Church. After their marriage in New York City, Arie found work as a seamstress and Luther became a shipping clerk.

The first few years of Colin's life were spent in a rough area of Harlem, and then his family moved to the melting-pot neighborhood called Banana Kelly in the South Bronx in the early 1940s.

BLESSED ARE THEY
WHO MAINTAIN
JUSTICE, WHO
CONSTANTLY DO
WHAT IS RIGHT.

PSALM 106:3 NIV

"My friends were Puerto Rican, Italian, and Greek," Powell says. "My entire life pretty much spanned a few blocks, with school on one end of Kelly Street, and my church, St. Margaret's Episcopal, on the other. Church was important in my family. We had our own pew, and I was even an altar boy. But after school, I headed to the Jewish center because both my parents worked, and it was a safe place for me."

The Christian faith was the cornerstone of the Powell family. They were all actively involved at St. Margaret's, where his mother was head of the altar guild, his father was senior warden and a lay reader, and his older sister, Marilyn, played the piano for the children's service. Colin was an acolyte and loved the pomp and circumstance of their formal worship, with its sweet smell of incense and the candles he got to light during the service. And when there was a church bazaar, or a bake sale, or a church-sponsored event, the Powell family attended and worked. Everyone was expected to take on some responsibility in serving the church.

One summer when he was in high school, Colin attended church camp and made some new friends who proved to be a bad influence. They talked him into sneaking out of camp with them to buy beer, and then they hid it in one of the toilet tanks to keep it cold. They thought no one would ever find out. But they were wrong.

The camp director called all the boys together to confront them with the fact that the beer had been discovered. The priest didn't yell or scream. He firmly asked the guilty parties to stand up and act like men and to accept the responsibility for their misdeed. Colin Powell, because of his mother's firm hand through his childhood years, was the one who came clean first.

"Father, I did it," Colin confessed.

Because of his honesty, two other boys also admitted their guilt. All of their parents were notified, and the boys were sent home in disgrace. Riding on the train, Colin thought about what he had done and regretted his involvement. How embarrassing for him and his parents! To get kicked out of church camp was worse than anything he could imagine.

After walking slowly home from the train, Colin was met at the door by his scowling mother. He stood silent as she lectured him about trust and responsibility, knowing there was no good defense for his actions. Then it was his father's turn to tell Colin how disappointed he was in his son.

In the middle of the family crisis, Father Weeden—the priest at St. Margaret's—called to tell Colin's parents the whole story—about how their son had stood up like a man and taken responsibility for his actions. Arie was proud that her Colin had done the right thing.

Because of his mother's influence in forming his character, Colin Powell became a trusted soldier and has been a valued and loyal advisor to presidents and other statesmen around the world. He served as National Security Advisor to President Ronald Reagan, became the first African American to serve as chairman of the Joint Chiefs of Staff under President George H. W. Bush, and in 2001 the U.S. Senate confirmed his appointment as Secretary of State under President George W. Bush. By carefully teaching her son to be a person of integrity, Arie Powell's influence was felt throughout the world.

**A Mother of Influence teaches
her children to do what is right.**

Cor Luitingh ten Boom

Unknown - 1919

CORRIE TEN BOOM. Cor ten Boom taught her daughter Corrie to treat all people with compassion—even her enemies.

༺∞༻

Corrie ten Boom's mother, Cor, for whom she was named, never knew a stranger. She was a warm, gentle, and compassionate woman of faith, a member of the Dutch Reform Church, who brought harmony and laughter to the ten Boom home and the ticking clock shop of her husband, Caspar.

For needy or neighborhood children, she provided a warm and loving place where freshly baked cookies awaited them on cold snowy days. For adults in need, it was a place of refuge where they could always find a meal. For friends and strangers alike, it was a house filled with music, laughter, and spirited conversation.

From the time Corrie was a small child, Cor ten Boom took her daughter along on her errands of mercy, where she might give solace to a new mother who had lost her baby or take a basket of food to someone homebound because of illness or infirmity.

Without depleting their own supply, Cor always managed to find enough to share with others. It was said that Corrie's mother had the gift for "stretching a guilder until it cried." There was always room for one more at the dinner table, even if Cor had to add water to the vegetable soup or split a piece of dark bread. No one was turned away hungry. Her mother's gift of hospitality shaped young Corrie's personality and prepared her for her life's work, ministering the love and compassion of

Christ to a suffering world.

After her mother's death in 1919, the ten Boom family spent the next decade opening their arms to numerous foster children—refugees, missionary kids, orphans. They also continued their Christian outreach in their community—ministering to girls, and embracing their Jewish neighbors who suffered under the cloud of anti-Semitism creeping ever closer.

> YOU SERVE ME A SIX-COURSE DINNER RIGHT IN FRONT OF MY ENEMIES. YOU REVIVE MY DROOPING HEAD; MY CUP BRIMS WITH BLESSING.
>
> PSALM 23:5 MSG

Thankfully, Corrie ten Boom's mother never had to suffer through the dark days of World War II and Hitler's occupation of Holland. When the Nazis invaded their homeland, the ten Booms carried on their Christian work, hiding their Jewish neighbors or members of the Dutch resistance who were being hunted by the Gestapo. Even though it placed them in great danger, they courageously fashioned a small hiding place in their home where they hid many from the Nazis.

Their network continued to grow until one day when it all came to a sudden end. Corrie, her sister Betsie, her father, and many others were arrested and carted off to concentration camps. Still the Gestapo never found the hiding place in the wall of Corrie's bedroom, or the six people sheltered in its tiny space.

Corrie's eighty-four-year-old father died within ten days of their arrest, and her beloved sister Betsie would also perish in the camps, but not before Corrie and Betsie suffered brutal treatment at the hands of their Nazi guards. Despite their inhumane treatment, these remarkable young women managed to conduct Bible studies in the camps, and many came to Christ.

After the war, Corrie had every right to be bitter, but instead, she traveled around the world telling her story and ministering the love, compassion, and forgiveness of Christ. She rarely stayed in hotels. Just as the ten Boom family had sheltered others, Christian families opened their homes to her.

"I think that I am enjoying the reward for the wide open doors and hearts of our home," Corrie said.

Years after her experience in a Nazi Germany concentration camp, Corrie ten Boom found herself standing face-to-face with one of the most cruel and heartless German guards she had ever met in the camps. This man had raped her and Betsie with his eyes as they stood naked in the delousing shower. Now he stood before her with an outstretched hand, asking, "Will you forgive me?"

"I stood there with coldness clutching at my heart," Corrie said, "but I know that the will can function regardless of the temperature of the heart. I prayed, 'Jesus, help me!'

"Woodenly, mechanically, I thrust my hand into the one stretched out to me, and I experienced an incredible thing. The current started in my shoulder, raced down into my arm, and sprang into our clutched hands. Then this warm reconciliation seemed to flood my whole being, bringing tears to my eyes. 'I forgive you, brother,' I cried with my whole heart. For a long moment we grasped each other's hands, the former guard, the former prisoner. I have never known the love of God so intensely as I did in that moment!"

Corrie ten Boom's mother gave her not only the tools to survive a Nazi concentration camp, but she gave her the tools to live the rest of her life in triumph, inspiring millions of people with her story.

A Mother of Influence instructs and encourages her children to extend compassion to others.

SUSANNAH ANNESLEY WESLEY

1669 - 1742

JOHN AND CHARLES WESLEY. Susannah Wesley

taught her sons the power of prayer.

⚜

I t was time to pray. A woman of strong opinions and convictions, Susannah Wesley knelt, her Bible in hand, and pulled the large apron over her head. Her children knew not to interrupt her for the next hour. This was their mother's daily time alone with God—time to seek His face and intercede for her children—and her routine never wavered.

Unlike the old woman in the shoe from the Mother Goose rhyme, Susannah knew exactly how she wanted to raise her children. The mother of nineteen (only nine survived to adulthood) spent at least one hour a day praying for each and every one of them. But that wasn't the end of it. Susannah also made time to set aside an hour during the week with each of her children to focus only on that one child and to discuss spiritual matters. It was a disciplined household that ran like a finely tuned clock.

Susannah once wrote, "I insist upon conquering the child's will early on. Self-will is the root of all sin and misery, so whatever cherishes this in children ensures their after-wretchedness. Whatever checks and mortifies it, promotes their future happiness and piety. When we consider that religion is doing the will of God and not our own, the one grand impediment to our temporal and eternal happiness is this self-will. Thus, no indulgence of it can be trivial, no denial unprofitable.

"Heaven or hell depends on this alone; so that the parent who studies

[JESUS SAID,] "WITH GOD ALL THINGS ARE POSSIBLE."

MATTHEW 19:26 NASB

to subdue self-will in his child, works together with God in the renewing and saving of a soul. The parent who indulges the child's self-will does the devil's work, makes religion impracticable, salvation unattainable, and does all that in him lies, to damn his child, soul and body, forever."

It was not an easy life. Susannah's husband, Samuel, was poorly paid as the rector of St. Andrew's Church in Epworth, Lincolnshire, England, and was often away from home. It was left up to her to steer their children down a path of righteousness, while at the same time making sure the food stretched to feed all their hungry little mouths. But she never wavered. The London-born mother also found time to homeschool her children for six hours each day, teaching them literature, music, mathematics, science, Latin, Greek, and theology.

Having grown up with her minister father (a Puritan) and known religious persecution, Susannah wanted her life to count for God. As a child, she prayed that He would use her to light a spiritual fire in England that would spread around the world. He did, but not in the way she imagined. Instead, God called Susannah to serve as a mother, and it would be her son John, an ordained Anglican priest, who would experience a spiritual awakening and launch the Methodist movement. And her son Charles, also an Anglican priest, would give the church more than 9,000 cherished hymns.

Samuel Wesley once told his wife that "some of the truly great people are the ones who were faithful in doing little things." There is no doubt it was Susannah's "little" prayers that changed the world.

A Mother of Influence teaches her children to pray.

CAROLINE LAKE (QUINER) INGALLS

1839 - 1924

LAURA INGALLS WILDER. Caroline Ingalls taught her daughter,

Laura, who would one day write about her childhood

in *The Little House* books, to find joy in life.

⌐❦⌐

"It is still best to be honest and truthful," once wrote Laura Ingalls Wilder, "to make the most of what we have; to be happy with simple pleasures and to be cheerful and have courage when things go wrong."

How did Laura acquire her life's philosophy? Her mother—"Ma"—was the rock of the Ingalls family. Caroline Quiner Ingalls provided the stability in their lives, teaching her girls to be ladies, even when they were moving from place to place in the Wild West. Ma and the girls all loved Pa—Charles Ingalls, a pioneer with a ready story on his tongue and wanderlust in his heart—and they would follow him anywhere, even into Indian territory. Ma was a pioneer woman, just as her husband was a pioneer man.

Schooling for the Ingalls family was sporadic at best. Ma always wanted to stay in one place and let the girls attend school, but very often they settled in places where no schoolhouse had yet been established. When that happened, she taught her children herself. Reading and writing were important, as was learning how to smoke a hog after it was butchered. The wisdom she passed on to her family was practical. Gentle, hard-working Ma did whatever was necessary to help her family survive with grace, whether it was sewing or gardening or cooking. She taught

MY CHILD, NEVER
FORGET THE THINGS
I HAVE TAUGHT
YOU. STORE MY
COMMANDS IN YOUR
HEART, FOR THEY
WILL GIVE YOU A
LONG AND SATISFY-
ING LIFE.

PROVERBS 3:1-2 NLT

them to make do with what they had and to be grateful for it.

Laura's childhood experiences on the prairie were a part of American history that begged to be written down, but it would be 1931 before Laura began writing the "faction-al" Little House book series. Ma was gone by then. But Laura's rich memories were still alive. She began to write with the goal of preserving the wonderful stories of her family and the settlement of this country. Surprisingly to her, the books were an instant success.

All of the Little House books, except for Farmer Boy, won the prestigious Newberry Medal for best children's literature. The American Library Association established the Laura Ingalls Wilder Award in 1954, making Laura the first recipient, and her books continue to be republished and read by new audiences every year. The books even inspired a hit TV series produced by Michael Landon.

It would not have occurred to Laura or her Ma that she would achieve fame. They were more practical than that. But readers of all ages and in more than forty countries have been eager to read about Laura's family —her sweet Ma— her fiddle-playing Pa— and the little houses of her past. Because Ma taught her daughter to find joy in the simple things of life, her pioneer spirit continues to inspire people of all ages.

A Mother of Influence knows joy can be found in the simple rhythm of life.

ANN MARIA REEVES JARVIS

1832 - 1905

ANNA JARVIS. By living an exemplary life of service to others,

Anna Maria Reeves Jarvis inspired her daughter Anna

as the founder of Mother's Day.

⁍⧜⁌

The Civil War continued to rage, and casualties mounted. It tore at the heart of Ann Maria Reeves Jarvis, a daughter of West Virginia. She lived in a border state between the North and South and witnessed daily how the war had divided families. Men fought in uniform, but women could only bind their wounds. Mrs. Jarvis spent most of the war years organizing women to nurse those wounded soldiers—no matter on which side they fought.

After the war, her work was not done. She launched "Mothers' Friendship Days" to bring reconciliation to families who had been deeply divided by their loyalties. The spiritual wounds of brother fighting brother ran deep. Only a mother could look past the politics and bind a broken heart.

Giving of her time and tireless support was only one of the many sacrifices Mrs. Jarvis would make in her lifetime. She had dreams of attending college, but instead, she gave them up to nurse an older husband and four children. Seven other children had been lost to disease, yet she continued to stay active in benevolent work, teaching Sunday school for more than twenty years at the local Methodist church. Her Mothers' Day Work Clubs, which were started before the Civil War, were instrumental in working for more healthy and sanitary conditions, raising money for

HONOR YOUR FATHER AND MOTHER, WHICH IS THE FIRST COMMANDMENT WITH PROMISE: THAT IT MAY BE WELL WITH YOU AND YOU MAY LIVE LONG ON THE EARTH.

EPHESIANS 6:2-3 NKJV

medicine, taking care of women with tuberculosis, and initiating a drive for the inspection of milk and other food supplies.

When Mrs. Jarvis passed away in 1905, her daughter Anna was almost inconsolable. How could she ever thank her mother for all she had done in her lifetime? How could she thank all the mothers who had influenced her life? In 1907, Anna got an idea. Why not set up a holiday near Memorial Day to honor the efforts of her mother and others like her who had made contributions during the Civil War? Many had sent husbands or sons to fight, nursed strangers back to health, kept the home fires burning, and worked for peace. It was time to honor them as patriots, as well as mothers. Memorial Day had been proclaimed in 1868 to honor men who had made sacrifices to the war effort. Mother's Day would honor women who had made sacrifices just as great.

As World War I loomed on the horizon in 1914, the Congress and President Woodrow Wilson officially recognized Mother's Day. Through the years, it would fast become one of our country's most popular celebrations. Anna Jarvis planned the holiday to be spent quietly in church observances and at home, quite different from the celebrations we have today.

Anna started the tradition of giving a white carnation on Mother's Day because it was her mother's favorite flower. It was a huge success, so much so that there were not enough white carnations to go around. Florists began to encourage the giving of all types of flowers. By the 1920s, it was one of the most profitable holidays. Anna Jarvis wanted people to rebel and stop buying gifts to line the pockets of merchants, but she had little success.

Today, children are still paying tribute to their mothers with cards and flowers and phone calls—all because Mrs. Jarvis gave of herself to others, setting an example of godly service.

A Mother of Influence sets a godly example for her children.

MARY LITOGOT O'HERN FORD

1838 or 1839 - 1875

HENRY FORD. Mary Ford encouraged her son Henry to pursue his

mechanical interests, and as a result, he launched an automotive empire.

⚬⟨∞⟩⚬

Henry was Mary Ford's "born mechanic." He was different from most boys reared on the nearby Dearborn, Michigan, farms. As a boy, he was more enthralled with watches—taking them apart and putting them back together—than he was with mucking out stalls or plowing fields. He soon became known throughout the neighborhood as someone who could fix your watch if it was broken.

But he needed tools. Mother to the rescue! Mary's knitting needles were fashioned by Henry into screwdrivers, and her corset stays became tiny tweezers. Using these makeshift tools and the odd pocket watches he picked up here and there, he continued to pursue his passion.

Mary also taught Henry to be responsible and self-reliant, traits that would serve him well when she was gone. When Henry was only twelve, his beloved mother died, leaving him, he recalled later, "like a watch without a mainspring." But in those early formative years, she had encouraged him to find what he did best and do it.

As a teenager, the self-taught machinist and mechanic took off for Detroit, where he worked as an apprentice in a machine shop. The Industrial Revolution was sweeping the world, and Henry Ford was born at the right time and in the right place to ride the crest of its wave.

Other automobile manufacturers were building luxury cars for the elite, but Henry was inspired to put the common man on wheels. He

I DIDN'T SKIMP OR
TRIM IN ANY WAY.
EVERY TRUTH AND
ENCOURAGEMENT
THAT COULD HAVE
MADE A DIFFERENCE
TO YOU, YOU GOT.

ACTS 20:20 MSG

wanted to make life on the farm a little easier.

In 1903, Henry Ford and ten investors launched his own corporation, The Ford Motor Car Company. By 1913, he had pioneered the moving assembly line, which not only revolutionized car manufacturing but also was quickly adapted by other manufacturing companies. Now products could be produced more cheaply and uniformly.

"I will build a motor car for the great multitude," Henry Ford once said, "constructed of the best materials, by the best men to be hired, after the simplest designs that modern engineering can devise, so low in price that no man making a good salary will be unable to own one and enjoy with his family the blessing of hours of pleasure in God's great open spaces."

And he did just that. The Model T, also known as a Tin Lizzie, rolled out of his factory in 1908, and Ford dominated auto sales for the next eighteen years.

Perhaps one of the most revolutionary concepts was his institution in 1914 of the five-dollar wage for an eight-hour workday. It was unheard of and caused quite an uproar with other business owners. But Henry believed it was the right thing to do.

"There are thousands of men out there who are not living as they should," Ford said to his minister at the time. "What they need is the opportunity to do better and someone to take a little interest in them."

Everyone realizes the impact of Henry Ford's life on our lives today, but few may understand that it was his mother who set the stage for his accomplishments. Because she recognized and nurtured his natural abilities as a mechanic rather than steering him down the more traditional road toward agriculture, Henry was able to put the force of his talent and intellect behind a dream that would change our world forever.

A Mother of Influence encourages her children's natural abilities.

FELIKSA WALESA

Unknown

LECH WALESA. Feliksa Walesa passed on her great faith,

with its strong sense of justice, to her son Lech Walesa,

who would one day lead a national labor movement

and become the first freely elected

President of Poland in fifty years.

⸎

My mother "is the only person from my childhood I still have a really clear recollection of," Lech Walesa writes in his autobiography, *A Way of Hope*. "She took an interest in history and current affairs, and read a great deal. In the evenings, she would sometimes read to us. We took great pleasure in these moments. All the stories our mother told us had a moral in them: they taught one to be honest, to strive always to better oneself, to be just, and to call white white and black black. Mother was very religious. My faith can be said almost to have flowed into me with my mother's milk."

The parish priest of the village of Popow, between Warsaw and Gdansk, Poland, where Lech Walesa was born on September 29, 1943, called Feliksa "the wisest woman in the parish. She always had to be the most important person around and was a fantastic organizer. Lech is an extension of his mother and even looks like her. He has the same face, size, build and smile."

When Lech was born in a clay hut to Feliksa and carpenter Boleslaw Walesa, Nazi Germany's iron boot was firmly planted across the throat of Poland. Lech's father was conscripted by the occupiers to dig ditches, and in 1946 Boleslaw died as a result of exposure and the beatings he had suf-

[JESUS SAID,] "GOD BLESSES THOSE WHO ARE HUNGRY AND THIRSTY FOR JUSTICE, FOR THEY WILL RECEIVE IT IN FULL."

MATTHEW 5:6 NLT

fered, leaving Lech's mother to raise him and his three siblings. But Boleslaw's brother, who also had three children, had promised to take care of the family, and he kept his vow.

The children in the Walesa home were kept on a "tight rein," he recalls. Even the youngest had jobs to do—tending geese, taking the cows out to pasture, doing a variety of manual jobs. When Lech was ten years old, he had to walk five kilometers to school, and then seven kilometers after school to the Catholic church. It was a daily part of life.

In speaking of Poland, Walesa once said in an interview, "We could only survive as a nation thanks to our deep belief in God, because we lived through some absolutely hopeless situations in history, and on several occasions, we were erased as a country from the map of the world. But thanks to our religious belief, we survived."

As they had persevered through the Nazi occupation, so they survived the Cold War occupation by the Soviet Union. Even though it was forbidden, the family would huddle around a radio at night, listening to the broadcasts of Radio Free Europe and the BBC. They could have been thrown into jail had anyone discovered them.

As a child, Lech Walesa would have said he was not a political creature, yet he had learned to yearn for justice at his mother's knee. He hated the system of Soviet repression, and as a young man he began to speak out. As an electrician in the Lenin shipyard in Gdansk, he would become even more vocal about the injustice of the communist system. He helped organize the first labor union and was jailed many times for his efforts, but an unstoppable movement—Solidarity—had begun.

During the 1970s and 1980s, Walesa came to the attention of presidents, kings, and prime ministers and told them his belief that communism would fall peacefully. No one agreed with him until a Pole was elected Pope.

In an interview, Lech Walesa said, "We get this divine gift from Heaven, when nobody believes it's possible. Here we have a Pole becoming Pope. A year later he visits Poland and tells us, 'Don't be afraid. Change the face of this world.' And soon after, we stopped fearing. The fear is gone. A year later . . . out of the ten people that I had in my command at that point, I have ten million supporting me, and I actually carry out changing the face of the world."

Because his mother never compromised her values and instilled those beliefs in her son, Lech Walesa not only helped defeat communism in his country, he became Poland's first freely elected president in fifty years and went on to win the 1983 Nobel Peace Prize—proof of what a strong, believing mother's influence can do.

A Mother of Influence teaches her children the difference between right and wrong.

DRONDA BOJAXHIU

Unknown

MOTHER TERESA. Dronda Bojaxhiu laid a foundation for daughter Gonxha (Agnes) Bojaxhiu, better known as Mother Teresa, on which to build a selfless life.

◦◦◦◦◦◦◦◦◦

Mother Teresa never spoke much about her childhood, only to say that because it was a happy one, she felt called to a selfless life of service to the poor. Her brother Lazar once said that it was the example set by their mother, Dronda, who was always helping someone less fortunate, that inspired the young Gonxha to lay down her life for others as a nun.

Born August 27, 1910, in Skopje, Yugoslavia, to Nikola, a successful contractor, and his wife, Dronda, Gonxha lived in a community of some 20,000 people—a population half Muslim and half Christian. The family was devoted to the Catholic church, with prayer and church attendance as much a part of their day as breathing. Both Gonxha and her sister Aga sang in their local church choir, as well as the Skopje Albanian Youth Choir.

Some accounts say that as early as twelve years of age, Gonxha expressed her desire to her mother to become a nun, perhaps motivated by her mother's benevolence. Certainly, she was always interested in stories about world missionaries and their work and could point out their location on the map. Some say that it was not until she was in her late teens that the woman who would become known worldwide as Mother Teresa decided to pursue her calling to the church.

In any case, the family lived in material comfort until about 1919, when Gonxha's father died under sudden and mysterious circumstances.

It was suspected he was poisoned by political enemies. Overnight, life changed for Dronda and her three children. She was now solely responsible for their welfare, and the family drew closer.

At the age of eighteen, Gonxha followed her heart and traveled to Dublin, where she joined the Sisters of Loreto, an education and missions-oriented order founded in the seventeenth century to teach young girls. She would never again see her mother, the woman who had nurtured her with prayer and devotion during her childhood.

A year after moving to Dublin, Gonxha was sent to Darjeeling, India, as a novitiate of the Sisters of Loreto and took her final vows in 1931. She chose the name of Teresa in honor of two other saints of the church—Teresa of Avila and Therese of Lisieux.

Teresa's long years of service to God would begin as a high school teacher at St. Mary's in Calcutta. For the next fifteen years, she taught history and geography to wealthy young women.

> WHEN THE TIME CAME, HE [JESUS] SET ASIDE THE PRIVILEGES OF DEITY AND TOOK ON THE STATUS OF A SLAVE, BECAME HUMAN! HAVING BECOME HUMAN, HE STAYED HUMAN. IT WAS AN INCREDIBLY HUMBLING PROCESS. HE DIDN'T CLAIM SPECIAL PRIVILEGES. INSTEAD, HE LIVED A SELFLESS, OBEDIENT LIFE AND THEN DIED A SELFLESS, OBEDIENT DEATH—AND THE WORST KIND OF DEATH AT THAT: A CRUCIFIXION.
>
> PHILIPPIANS 2:7-8 MSG

In 1946, Teresa traveled to Darjeeling for a retreat, and it was there she received her "second calling." She felt God was telling her to give up her protected position with the Sisters of Loreto and minister to those who lived on the streets.

"I heard the call to give up all and follow Christ into the slums to serve Him among the poorest of the poor," she would say about the experience.

It was not easy. She had to convince the Archbishop of Calcutta to let her follow her heart into the streets. She would no longer live in safety and comfort, and she would exchange her nun's habit for the more practical sari worn by native women.

After taking a nursing course to prepare her for work among the sick, Teresa received permission in 1948 to live as an independent nun in the streets of Calcutta. Her home was little more than a hovel, and she began by teaching the children on the street. She had no school supplies other than the dust in which to write. Literacy was not the only subject she taught.

She also taught them basic hygiene, and once they trusted her, the girls took her to the homes of the poor and ill, where she offered her help. With little medicine to offer, prayer was her first offense against sickness.

Within a year of striking out on her own though, more help arrived. Young women came from everywhere to volunteer their services, and the Missionaries of Charity mushroomed. Food, clothes, and medical supplies also found their way to her doorstep. The group, with Mother Teresa as its head, reached out to lepers by opening treatment centers and hospitals, set up orphanages, treated alcoholics, and fed the poor. Those who sought aid also found love and compassion delivered with a smile.

Mother Teresa often said she was "God's pencil—a tiny bit of pencil with which He writes what He likes." She would take God's pencil around the world, drawing a portrait of His face for everyone she met, including kings, presidents, and world leaders.

Even after her death in 1997, the work of the Missionaries of Charity continues, in large part because her mother taught her by example to care for those less fortunate. Though Dronda did not live to see her daughter's work, those who struggle with poverty, disease, and hopelessness have felt her influence.

A Mother of Influence teaches her children to care about the needs of others.

ALBERTA WILLIAMS KING

1903 - 1974

MARTIN LUTHER KING JR. The daughter and wife of strong

Christian ministers, Alberta encouraged Martin's strength

of purpose in fighting racial inequality.

⚜

The precocious five-year-old M.L., as he was called, stood before his mother and recited a Scripture verse. Alberta praised her son, inoculating him with a strong sense of worth from childhood. They were black and living in segregated Atlanta, Georgia, but Alberta never wanted her son to feel inferior.

It was confusing though. Until they were of school age, M.L. and his white friends were allowed to play together, but after that, the ugly line of segregation was firmly drawn between them. After carefully explaining black history to her son, Alberta said, "You must never feel that you are less than anybody else. You must always feel that you are somebody."

M.L.'s father was pastor of the Ebenezer Baptist Church, so as an upper middle-class black, the young Martin Luther King Jr. never suffered economic want, but his clashes with the system of racial inequality filled him with anger and a determination to hate all white people.

King sailed through school, skipping grades, and graduated from Booker T. Washington High School at the age of fifteen. It was not until he entered Morehouse College and came into contact with white students on an intercollegiate council that he realized hating whites was inconsistent with his faith. Instead, he directed his anger at the system of segregation that fostered hatred between the races.

Prepared to change his world as a doctor or lawyer, King found his calling as a minister at Morehouse. After receiving a degree in sociology, the charismatic young man, who could hold an audience spellbound with his voice, entered Crozer Theological Seminary in Pennsylvania and graduated at the top of his class in 1951.

It was at Crozer that he was exposed to the writings of Walter Rauschenbusch, who espoused a socially relevant faith, and became interested in the teachings of Mahatma Gandhi and his philosophy of nonviolence and redemptive love as a means of social change.

"It is quite easy for me to think of a God of love," King wrote in an essay while at Crozer, "because I grew up in a family where love was central and where lovely relationships were ever present."

After receiving his Ph.D. in systematic theology while pastoring Dexter Avenue Baptist Church in Montgomery, Alabama, King assumed he would become a scholar and hoped to teach theology someday at the university level. But it was not God's will.

Instead, Martin Luther King Jr. would be used as a sharp instrument to surgically remove the cancer of racial segregation in this country. When Rosa Parks refused to give up her seat on a bus to a white passenger and sparked the civil rights revolution, King suddenly found himself as the leader of a nonviolent bus boycott, drawing on his faith to restore the races with love instead of hate. Quickly, King became the voice of freedom to blacks everywhere.

In 1957, he and 115 other black ministers formed the Southern Christian Leadership Conference, enlisting the support of black congregations around the South. The Christian faith had sustained them since the dark days of slavery, and now it would help them rise into a new dawn of liberty.

The rest of King's life would be filled with boycotts, sit-ins, marches, and protests against unjust segregation laws. He would spend time in jail for his beliefs, yet he would win the Nobel Peace Prize for his efforts. King's "I Have a Dream" speech at the Lincoln Memorial on August 28, 1963, would electrify the world and touch the heart of America. His words still ring in people's hearts today, years after his life was taken by an assassin's bullet.

King talked about becoming a martyr. It was not something he sought out, yet perhaps God was preparing him for what was to come. In a speech on April 3, 1968, the night before his assassination, he addressed an audience of 500 at the Mason Temple in Memphis, his words strangely prophetic.

"Like anybody," he said, "I would like to live a long life. Longevity has its place. But I'm not concerned about that now. I just want to do God's will. And He's allowed me to go up to the mountain, and I've looked over, and I've seen the promised land. I may not get there with you. But I want you to know tonight that we as a people will get to the promised land."

The Nobel Peace Prize winner did not live to see the fruit of his labors in the field of civil rights. However, his dream of an America where all children, regardless of color, would have a bright future, continues to inspire millions today.

Alberta King taught her son that he had inherent worth, and in so doing, she inspired millions to value themselves and others as equals in God's sight. Her influence, even today, is helping to shape the attitudes of all Americans.

> LOVE DOES NOT DEMAND ITS OWN WAY. LOVE IS NOT IRRITABLE, AND IT KEEPS NO RECORD OF WHEN IT HAS BEEN WRONGED. IT IS NEVER GLAD ABOUT INJUSTICE BUT REJOICES WHENEVER THE TRUTH WINS OUT.
>
> 1 CORINTHIANS 13:5-6 NLT

A Mother of Influence teaches her children to value themselves as children of God.

NANCY ELLIOTT EDISON

1810 - 1871

THOMAS ALVA EDISON. Schoolteacher Nancy Edison instilled a

lifelong love of reading in her son Thomas, who would one day

become a world-renowned inventor.

⚬✖⚬

A ddled. Retarded. Mentally inferior. Unable to learn. Thomas
Edison's primary teacher had no faith that the seven-year-old boy
was capable of learning anything. His mother vehemently dis-
agreed, so after three months, she withdrew him from school. Long before
homeschooling became an accepted practice, Nancy Elliott Edison, an
experienced teacher, determined to educate the youngest of her seven
children by herself and turned him into a voracious reader.

Although Edison wasn't very interested in mathematics, he loved to
read books on physics and chemistry, and by the age of ten, he had set up
a chemistry laboratory in the cellar where he conducted a variety of inno-
vative experiments. His mother encouraged his original thinking and
trusted him to experiment with poisonous chemicals. Despite the alarmed
predictions of the neighborhood, he never blew up the house and was
actually quite admired for his pluck.

An entrepreneur by the age of twelve, Edison worked for the Grand
Trunk Railroad that ran between his home of Port Huron, Michigan, and
Detroit, selling food, tobacco, and newspapers to passengers. The young
Edison even set up a small printing press in one of the empty baggage
cars, selling subscriptions to his own newspaper "The Weekly Herald" for
eight cents a month. When he wasn't selling newspapers, he was experi-
menting in a small lab he had built on the train.

During the layovers in Detroit, Edison spent a great deal of time reading at the public library and developed the habit of sleeping only about four hours a day. Later in life Edison would say that he read every book he could find. "I didn't read a few books," he said. "I read the library."

At all the train stops along the way, Edison made friends with the telegraph operators, who taught him about electrical communication and how to operate a telegraph. In 1863, he became a telegraph operator himself and plied his trade throughout the Midwest, learning all he could from the people he met. By the age of sixteen, he was an inventor, discovering new labor-saving techniques for the telegraph that allowed him more time to read.

> [JESUS SAID,] "ANYONE WHO LISTENS TO MY TEACHING AND OBEYS ME IS WISE, LIKE A PERSON WHO BUILDS A HOUSE ON SOLID ROCK."
>
> MATTHEW 7:24 NLT

Members of the House of Representatives were the skeptical audience for a demonstration of Edison's first patented invention in 1868 of an "electronic vote recorder," which was designed to speed up the voting process in Congress. Members of the House were not interested in speeding up the voting process so Edison vowed he would never again invent something without investigating whether there was a "commercial demand" for it.

At the young age of twenty-three, Thomas Edison sold his first invention—a "universal stock ticker"—to General Lefferts, who was the head of Gold and Stock Telegraph Co., thinking he might make as much as $5,000. Lefferts instead offered Edison $40,000. The young inventor managed to stammer that the offer seemed fair and used his windfall to set up his first business.

Nicknamed "The Wizard of Menlo Park," a total of 1,093 patents would be issued to Thomas Edison in the course of his lifetime—more than any other individual in American history—and he was the only person to ever have a patent issued every year for sixty-five consecutive years. Some of his more famous inventions included the incandescent light bulb, an automatic telegraphy machine, the phonograph, a motion picture machine, and the discovery of the emission of electrons from a heated cathode—a phenomenon known as the Edison effect. Throughout his career, he credited his success to his mother.

Thomas Edison once wrote, "I did not have my mother long, but she cast over me a good influence that lasted all my life. The good effects of her training I can never lose. If it had not been for her appreciation and her faith in me at a critical time in my experience, I should never likely have become an inventor. I was always a careless boy, and with a mother of a different caliber, I should have turned out badly. But her firmness, her sweetness, her goodness, were potent powers to keep me in the right path. My mother was the making of me." Later he added, "Mothers have a way of shaping the future by the influence they have over their children."

By believing in his God-given potential and developing in him a desire to read, Edison's mother laid the foundation for her son's future success as the inventor who would light up the world.

A Mother of Influence has faith in her children's potential.

ANN REILLY GIBSON

Unknown - 1990

MEL COLUMCILLE GERARD GIBSON, A devout Catholic, Ann

Gibson taught her son the tenets of the faith that would later influence his

highly successful film The Passion of the Christ.

◦✕◦

For Mel Columcille (Gaelic for "dove of the church") Gibson, his film The Passion of the Christ is a personal journey in remembering the truth of his faith taught at his mother's knee.

Mel Gibson, the sixth of eleven children born to Hutton and Ann Gibson, grew up in a devoutly religious Roman Catholic family, but like many young people, he drifted away from his roots. Because his father feared his sons would be drafted for service in Vietnam, the railroad brake worker moved his family to Australia in 1968 when Mel was twelve years old. At first, he attended a Catholic boys school but was later moved to Asquith High School, a state-run school. At sixteen, he developed a fondness for smoking cigarettes and drinking beer.

At the age of seventeen, as Mel moved into adulthood, his rebellion increased, and he strayed from his family's faith. It would be eighteen years before he would have a profound and personal experience of the risen Lord that would bring him back home.

Once known as a bad boy of Hollywood—a two-fisted drinker and dubbed "The Sexiest Man Alive"—Mel Gibson seemed to be the least likely of men to tackle the story of Christ's passion. But it should not have come as a great surprise that God would use a flawed human being to illuminate Christ's sacrifice on the cross. As Gibson likes to say, he is still a "work in progress."

Gibson readily admits that in his mid-thirtiess, at the height of his fame and fortune, he was drowning in alcohol and near suicidal depression.

> **"THE LIFE OF THE FLESH IS IN THE BLOOD, AND I HAVE GIVEN IT TO YOU UPON THE ALTAR TO MAKE ATONEMENT FOR YOUR SOULS; FOR IT IS THE BLOOD THAT MAKES ATONEMENT FOR THE SOUL."**
>
> LEVITICUS 17:11 NKJV

None of the trappings of success had brought him happiness. Nor had a stable marriage with his wife, Robyn, and his many children. Finally, he fell on his knees and cried out to God for help and forgiveness. Gibson credits Jesus' sacrifice on the cross, taking on the sins of humanity, with saving his life.

In an interview with *The New Yorker*, Gibson said, "I had to use the Passion of Christ and His wounds to heal my wounds." In 1991, he joined Alcoholics Anonymous and returned to his Catholic traditionalist roots. He is an adherent to the faith of some 100,000 others in the U.S. who reject Vatican II and its modernizing reforms. His wife—an Episcopalian—and his seven children (ages 4 to 23) now attend Holy Family Chapel, a church Gibson had built near their Malibu, California, home.

A dozen years after his dramatic spiritual change and after on-the-job training as the director of such movies as *Braveheart*, Gibson was finally prepared to tackle the story of Christ's passion. He believes the film reveals the healing he himself received because of Jesus' blood sacrifice on the cross and claims that the film was really directed by the Holy Spirit. "I was only directing traffic," Gibson said.

When some of his detractors accuse Gibson of making an anti-Semitic film, Gibson is quick to stress that all of humanity's sins were responsible for the death of Jesus. To underscore that point, Gibson's own hands were filmed nailing Christ to the cross. "I'm first on line for culpability," Gibson said. "I did it." The Passion of the Christ opened in more than 4,600 theaters on Ash Wednesday, 2004, and has become one of the most successful films ever made.

With eleven children to raise, no one would have faulted Ann Gibson if she had simply found herself stretched too thin to instruct her children concerning the gospel of Christ and the things of God. Still, she found the time and energy to make sure that those precious seeds were deeply implanted in each of their hearts. The result is that millions now have a deeper understanding of Christ's sacrifice.

A Mother of Influence passes on to her children the tenets of her faith.

Sonya Copeland Carson

1928 (?) -

DR. BEN SOLOMON CARSON. Sonya Carson's belief

that her son Ben needed to aspire to higher academic goals

lifted him out of the ghetto and into the medical field,

where he became a world-renowned pediatric neurosurgeon.

⌇∞⌇

S onya Carson frowned at her son Ben's mid-term report card. He
tried to defend his poor grades, saying they didn't mean a lot. His
mother didn't buy it.

"If you keep making grades like this," she said, "you'll spend the rest
of your life sweeping floors in a factory. And that's not what God wants
for you!"

She pulled Ben and his brother Curtis close to her and said, "Boys, I
don't know what to do. But God promises in the Bible to give wisdom to
those who ask. So tonight I'm going to pray for wisdom. I am going to
ask God what I need to do to help you."

On the face of it, overcoming racism and rising out of poverty seemed
impossible. Sonya Carson was a single mom who had married at the age
of thirteen and divorced her husband when she found out he was a
bigamist. One of twenty-four children, Sonya had only a third-grade education and worked two and three jobs as a maid to feed her two boys. But
despite her circumstances, Sonya did not believe in the victim mentality
and knew God would hear her prayers.

YOU ARE THE ONES
CHOSEN BY GOD,
CHOSEN FOR THE
HIGH CALLING OF
PRIESTLY WORK, CHO-
SEN TO BE A HOLY
PEOPLE, GOD'S
INSTRUMENTS TO DO
HIS WORK AND SPEAK
OUT FOR HIM, TO
TELL OTHERS OF THE
NIGHT-AND-DAY DIF-
FERENCE HE MADE
FOR YOU—FROM
NOTHING TO SOME-
THING, FROM REJECT-
ED TO ACCEPTED.

1 PETER 2:9-10 MSG

Two days later, the young mother gathered her boys together and gave them her answer. "God says we need to turn off the television," Sonya said. "You may choose two TV shows to watch each week. We'll spend the rest of the time reading. You are also to write two book reports every week about the books you read. Then you can read your reports out loud to me."

Ben Carson and his brother were horri-fied. They tried to object, but their mother's mind was made up. Education was the way out for her boys. God had said it, and she believed it. The boys were allowed to choose the books they would read, according to their interests, but read they would.

"Initially, this course of action was quite distasteful to me," Dr. Carson said, "but I found it extremely beneficial in the long run. I learned that through the use of books, I had the whole world at my feet and could travel anywhere, meet anyone, and do virtually anything. I developed a vora-cious appetite for reading, and it was soon afterward that I discovered my intellectual potential."

Once a failing student, the fifth-grade boy was soon making straight A's. It wasn't easy, but Ben's mother never let him make excuses. She would say, "You have a brain, so think your way out of problems."

Excelling in high school, Ben Carson won a scholarship to Yale University, where he met Candy Ruskin. The two were married in 1975. He attended medical school at the University of Michigan in Ann Arbor and was accepted in the neurosurgery program at the prestigious Johns Hopkins University Medical School in Baltimore. At the age of thirty-three, he became the youngest chief of pediatric neurosurgery in the United States and went on to become its director. Dr. Ben Carson gained a world-renowned reputation when he separated Siamese twins joined at the head and treated children with severe seizure disorders by performing hemispherectomies, which involved removing half of the brain.

"I believe my mother demonstrates that parents—even single par-ents—can have a tremendous positive influence on their children," Dr.

Carson said. "My mother guided my brother Curtis, now a successful engineer living in Indiana, and me to adulthood by creating a disciplined, but loving, environment in which we could grow and learn. And she provided a good example by completing her high school equivalency exam and going on to junior college." Later Sonya Carson also received an honorary doctoral degree.

"I know God had a hand in all these events," Dr. Carson said, "just as I know He has had a hand in shaping everything good in my life. Thanks to God and a courageous mother, a poor kid from the streets of Detroit has been able to take part in medical miracles."

A Mother of Influence asks God for wisdom as she seeks to help each of her children reach his or her unique potential.

ELIZABETH NEWTON

Unknown - 1732

JOHN NEWTON. A godly woman who died of consumption just

thirteen days before her son John's seventh birthday,

Elizabeth Newton's influence reached into his adulthood

and gave him faith at his greatest time of need.

⌑

As if she somehow knew that she would never live to see her only child, John, grow into adulthood, the fragile Elizabeth Newton dedicated her short life to his education, praying fervently that he would one day become a minister of the Gospel. By the age of four, thanks to his mother's teaching methods, John Newton was reading the Bible and reciting hymns from Divine and Moral Songs for Children by Isaac Watts. Hand in hand, they attended an Independent (Congregational) church in London, a dissenting Puritan-derived group.

Despite her fierce love and loyalty to her son, Elizabeth finally released her hold on life and died of consumption shortly before John turned seven, and with her death his spiritual education ended. His father, a sea captain, soon remarried, and John was shipped off to boarding school, where he excelled as a student. At the age of ten, he was reading Latin and showed great potential in the field of mathematics. But his life would soon take another sharp turn.

When he was eleven years old, John Newton's father took him to sea, and for the next six years the young man made several voyages. Between trips, he stayed with his stepmother, who allowed him to run wild. Influenced by an environment filled with rough sailors while he was onboard ship and lax discipline at home, John's normal teenage rebellion was soon out of hand.

At the age of seventeen, he met Mary Catlett at her parents' estate in Kent. He was so smitten with her that the young seaman missed boarding a Jamaica-bound ship on which he was supposed to sail. His father was furious and decided to teach him a lesson. Always before, his father had watched over John. This time, the young man was put on a ship bound for Venice without the protection of his father. As a common seaman, he soon took up smoking, drinking, and swearing. Following a spiritual dream one night, he separated himself from his companions and returned to his childhood faith, but it wouldn't last.

> BY THE GRACE OF GOD I AM WHAT I AM: AND HIS GRACE WHICH WAS BESTOWED UPON ME WAS NOT IN VAIN; BUT I LABOURED MORE ABUNDANTLY THAN THEY ALL: YET NOT I, BUT THE GRACE OF GOD WHICH WAS WITH ME.
>
> 1 CORINTHIANS 15:10 KJV

Sometime later, when he was press-ganged onto a Royal Navy ship, John Newton's spiritual life faded to an undetectable flame. Under the influence of the captain's clerk, a man named Mitchell, John Newton gave up the God of his mother. Not satisfied to simply stray from her teachings, he also enjoyed persuading others to give up their faith.

Eventually, John Newton became a slave trader, trafficking in the misery of other human beings and living a dissipated life. On March 31, 1748, while sailing from Brazil to Newfoundland, his slave ship encountered a violent storm. The ship was in poor repair and began to take on water.

"Tied to the ship to prevent being washed away," Newton "pumped and bailed all night until he was called upon to steer the ship. All the while he reviewed his life: his former professions of religion, the extraordinary twists of past events, the warnings and deliverances he had met with, his licentious conversation, and his mockery of the Gospels."

At first, because of his many sins, Newton thought his life unworthy to be saved by God's grace. The storm raged on, the waves swept over the deck, and finally, Newton breathed his first small prayer in many years. He would say later that it was "the hour he first believed," a line he would use years later when he wrote the famous hymn "Amazing Grace." When they found safety on an island, Newton crept away and knelt between some palm trees, giving his life back to God. He never went back on his faith. Some time later, while suffering from a strange fever, he asked God to help him better understand the Christian faith and leave the slave trade. God heard his prayers. He sent him a Christian friend, whose words "inflamed" his heart, and he never sailed again. Instead, Newton gradually became an active lay person, teaching and preaching all over England. Later he would become an ordained Anglican priest, with his own parish, and in his later years, would serve and preach in one of the most prestigious churches in London.

"Amazing Grace," a hymn that has touched millions of hearts since it was first written, could be called John Newton's theme song. On his gravestone, his epitaph reads: "John Newton, clerk, once an infidel and libertine, a servant of slaves in Africa, was, by the rich mercy of our Lord and Saviour Jesus Christ, preserved, restored, pardoned, and appointed to preach the faith he had long laboured to destroy." A friend, Richard Cecil, quoted Newton at his funeral mass saying, "Whatever I may doubt on other points, I cannot doubt whether there has been a certain gracious transaction between God and my soul."

Despite the fact that she had only six years to influence her son, Elizabeth Newton's prayers were heard, her early instruction in the faith rewarded, and her dreams for a son who would preach the Gospel fulfilled. No matter how brief, the influence of a godly mother cannot be forgotten.

A Mother of Influence lets her children hear her singing the songs of her faith.

BONITA GRACE THOMPSON JENKINS

1926 -

JERRY JENKINS. Bonita Jenkins taught her son Jerry to be generous

with God's blessings, and when he became a best-selling author, he

remembered the lessons she had taught him.

⚜

One Christmas morning, Jerry and his brothers tore into their presents and played nonstop for about three days until they were bored. Then their mother, Bonita, carried an empty cardboard box into the dining room and called her boys together. The conversation centered on the local orphanage for boys and how all they got for Christmas was a small piece of fruit, a candy bar, a comb, and a cheap toy.

In telling the story, Jerry wrote how one of his brothers said with sarcasm, "Merry Christmas."

Exactly Bonita's point. She suggested they give those orphans a Christmas they would never forget.

"Let's fill this box with toys that will make Christmas special," Jerry relates his mother said. "We'll do what Jesus would do."

One of his brothers thought that it would be good to give away all his old toys to the orphans since he had new toys. Jerry said his brother ran to his room and gathered up a bunch of old beat-up toys. Quietly, Bonita Jenkins asked, "Is that what Jesus would do?"

One of his brothers asked her, "You want us to give our new stuff?"

"It's just a suggestion," she said.

"All of it?"

"I didn't have in mind all of it," their mother said. "Just whatever toys you think."

"I'll give this car," one of the Jenkins boys offered.

"If you don't want that," a brother said, "I'll take it."

The squabble over toys continued, with someone else wanting one of the old toys when the other brother was willing to give it up for the orphans. None of them noticed when their mother left the room.

"The box sat there, empty and glaring," Jerry writes. They all went back to playing with their new toys on the floor, "but there was none of the usual laughing, arguing, roughhousing."

Soon, one by one, the boys went in search of their mother and found her in the small kitchen. Dressed in her winter hat and coat, she sat at the table, waiting for Jerry and his brothers to do the right thing.

"Her face had that fighting tears look," Jerry writes, but she didn't nag or pressure them to give up their toys. She didn't have to say anything. Bonita Jenkins had taught her boys to share, and she knew they eventually would.

Jerry and his brothers quietly went back to playing with their new toys in the middle of the floor, as if they were saying good-bye to them. Then they returned to the box and gave up their best toys for the orphan boys who otherwise would have received so little. When they were finished giving, Mrs. Jenkins returned for the box and took it to the car.

Jerry said his mother never told them how the toys had been received at the orphanage, and he and his brothers never asked. It was not important. They had been taught a more important lesson about giving to others.

In the early days of his career in Michigan, Jerry Jenkins worked as a journalist and publishing executive before turning to writing "as told to" biographies for Christian evangelicals such as Billy Graham. Fiction was always his first love though, but he wrote nonfiction to pay the bills. Finally, his publishing dreams came true, and he became the successful author of a young adult mystery series and then the 60-million selling Left Behind series. Jenkins has written more than one hundred books in his career. He and Tim LaHaye are the cocreators of the phenomenally successful apocalyptic novels in the Left Behind series, with sales rivaling the books of John Grisham or Stephen King. Despite financial success, money has never been the driving force in Jerry's life. Ministry is more important to him than money. He calls himself "the most famous writer no one's ever heard of."

Jenkins has never lost sight of his belief that the blessings of God are given to bless others in return, so he shares his good fortune by mentoring other writers through the Christian Writers Guild. Those who know him will tell you he is a humble and approachable man, who still lives by the values his mother instilled in him as a young boy.

Jenkins remembers how his mother would turn the pages of her old King James Bible (one he would sometimes scribble in when she wasn't looking) for him until he could read it himself.

One of her favorite Bible verses was Psalm 37:4, which reads, "Delight thyself also in the Lord; and he shall give thee the desires of thine heart."

Jenkins once wrote that it was the desire of her heart that "her little boys would grow up and do something more profitable with those once small hands. Mom's first desire, she told us, was that her four boys would make decisions to trust Christ. We have all done that. Mom still delights herself in the Lord, which is a continual encouragement for me to do something constructive with the hands that scribbled in her Bible so many years ago."

> [JESUS SAID,] "I TELL YOU, USE YOUR WORLDLY RESOURCES TO BENEFIT OTHERS AND MAKE FRIENDS. IN THIS WAY, YOUR GENEROSITY STORES UP A REWARD FOR YOU IN HEAVEN."
>
> LUKE 16:9 NLT

A Mother of Influence sets an example of generosity.

FANNIE STUBBLEFIELD

Unknown

DR. RUTH SIMMONS. Fannie Stubblefield, a sharecropper

and the grandchild of a slave, taught her daughter Ruth,

who would one day become the eighteenth president

of Brown University, to always do her best.

⟡

Steam rose from the white man's long-sleeved dress shirt, bathing Fannie Stubblefield's face in sweat. Despite the heat, she carefully ironed the collar stiff and flattened the puckered material around each button. Ruth watched and wondered how her mother could be so meticulous after scrubbing houses all day. She must have been tired, yet she took the time to make sure the shirt was ironed perfectly smooth. It was a lesson Ruth would always remember: no matter how humble the job, always do your best.

Born July 3, 1945, in Grapeland, Texas, the twelfth child of share-croppers Fannie and Isaac Stubblefield, Ruth was soon toddling behind her parents and siblings in the blistering East Texas sun, carrying the empty sacks that the rest of the family would fill with cotton.

When she was seven, before she was old enough to pick cotton, the family left the fields behind and moved to the tiny house on Sumpter Street in one of Houston's roughest neighborhoods—the Fifth Ward. Her father initially took a job in a factory, but later became a minister at the Mount Hermon Missionary Baptist Church. It was in Houston that Ruth's mother would start her years of servitude as a domestic, cleaning other people's houses and doing their ironing. It was the accepted future for young black women.

"The neighborhoods I grew up in were brutally segregated and enforced, of course, by law in the world I grew up in," Dr. Ruth Simmons has written. "The boundary between black and white was absolute; the possibility of crossing it was not in my comprehension."

In speaking of her parents, Dr. Simmons once told a *Time* magazine interviewer, "They worked from sunup to late evening, and my mother took in ironing. I was so moved as a child when she had to work all day to earn enough money for a pair of shoes for me."

WE ARE HIS WORK-MANSHIP, CREATED IN CHRIST JESUS FOR GOOD WORKS, WHICH GOD PREPARED BEFOREHAND THAT WE SHOULD WALK IN THEM.

EPHESIANS 2:10 NKJV

"I was intent on doing something productive and on being everything my parents taught me to be," wrote Dr. Simmons in her essay, "My Mother's Daughter: Lessons I Learned in Civility and Authenticity" published in the Texas Council for the Humanities Journal in Spring-Summer 1998. "Their values were clear: do good work; don't ever get too big for your breeches; always be an authentic person; don't worry too much about being famous and rich because that doesn't amount to too much."

Ruth's mother taught her that rising out of poverty would be difficult, but not impossible. The key to success was a strong work ethic, and the door was a good education. Fannie often encouraged her children with stories of others who had overcome racism and risen to success. It could be done.

Although her mother died when Ruth was only fifteen, the young girl never gave up hope and continued to study long and hard. Ruth's teachers encouraged her to strive for a higher education, despite the fact that very few black students from her neighborhood ever attended college. But Ruth Simmons excelled academically and graduated as the salutatorian of her high school class.

When she was accepted to Dillard University in New Orleans and granted scholarships, Ruth's teachers acted as surrogate mothers, sending her money and even buying her clothes when needed.

"These were people that wanted me to succeed in the worst possible way," she once wrote. "They knew the odds out there, and wanted me to overcome them." And overcome she did, graduating from Dillard in 1967 summa cum laude.

Eventually, Ruth Simmons received her Ph.D. from Harvard University in romance languages, and from there, she went on to

Princeton where she served as associate dean of the faculty. Now as the first African-American president of Brown University, Dr. Simmons leads the Ivy League university with a humble respect for all people, remembering her sharecropper roots and realizing from her years of study and world travel that humanity is flawed.

"We all face the same great challenge," she relates, "to try to learn how to overcome the uncivilized instincts that come so naturally to us, instincts to distrust, belittle, and attack anyone who is different."

Dr. Simmons concludes that "we can learn respect for others no matter how different they are from us. We can learn and teach our children as my mother did—how to cherish our individual and collective integrity, even in the face of brutality."

By transcending and learning from her past, Dr. Simmons has proven the power of a mother's influence.

A Mother of Influence teaches her children to do their best.

LEAH POSNER
SPIELBERG ADLER

Unknown

STEVEN SPIELBERG. Leah Spielberg allowed her son Steven's imagination to soar free and encouraged the future filmmaker's creativity.

◦✄◦

Once when a teenaged Steven Spielberg needed to film a certain special effect with his 8mm camera, his mother, Leah, stuffed thirty cans of cherry pie filling into her pressure cooker and heated it until it exploded the mess all over her kitchen walls and ceiling. Months later, she was still cleaning cherry juice off her cupboards.

Most mothers would have nipped the future filmmaker's creativity in the bud and sent him to his room. Not so Leah. If her oldest child, Steven, needed an extra soldier in one of his early film epics, she would don a helmet over her blond hair and tear across the desert in her war surplus jeep.

Leah's willingness to nurture his creative talent forged a special bond between Steven and his mother, an accomplished pianist. For instance, when his early homemade films needed scoring, it was Leah who played the piano for dramatic effect.

From the age of twelve or thirteen, Steven Spielberg knew he wanted to be a movie director. He always had a knack for getting his friends and family, especially his mother and three younger sisters, to cooperate as actors, extras, or stunt people in his films. In fact, he credits his success to his whole family's willingness to help him. His first film shot in the seventh grade (in a real plane) was called Fighter Pilot and made use of real World War II footage.

Although Steven was born in Cincinnati, Ohio, on December 18,

1946, in a Jewish neighborhood, he would not grow up there. Because his father worked for the computer industry, they frequently relocated to take advantage of job opportunities.

"Just as I'd become accustomed to a school and a teacher and a best friend," Spielberg said in a *Time* magazine interview, "the FOR SALE sign would dig into the front lawn and we'd be packing and off to some other state. I've often considered Arizona, where I was from [age] nine to sixteen, my real home. For a kid, home is where you have best friends and your first car, and your first kiss; it's where you do your worst stuff and get your best grades."

It was not easy for a Jewish boy—sometimes the only one in his school—growing up in Christian neighborhoods and being teased for it. Steven admits he was a bit of a "nerd." He hated school and couldn't see any point in studying math or science when his ambition was to be a film director.

By high school, Steven's filmmaking "hobby" consumed his every waking hour. His entire junior year in Phoenix was spent making a full-length feature film called Firelight, the story of aliens abducting earthlings for an extraterrestrial zoo. Sometimes he would even fake being sick so he could stay home from school and work on editing the film. Leah knew what he was up to, but she allowed it.

"My house was a total studio," Leah told author Susan Goldman Rubin for her book *Steven Spielberg*. "Steve came along and took my house away. And the next thing on the menu was scaffolding, gel lights, a dolly."

She recognized his burning desire to be a moviemaker, and her support would pay off later. His popular films, including movies such as *Jaws*, *Raiders of the Lost Ark*, and *Close Encounters of the Third Kind*, have earned more than a billion dollars at the box office.

At the age of sixteen, the family moved again to northern California, where Leah and Steven's father, Arnold, finally separated and were later divorced. It had a profound effect on Spielberg, and some say his movie *E.T. the Extra-Terrestrial*, which became the top-grossing film of all time, mirrors the emotions he felt as a child.

But he is not bitter. He told *Time* magazine, "I have two wonderful parents; they raised me really well. Sometimes parents can work together to raise a wonderful family and not have anything in common with each other. That happens a lot in America."

Although his poor grades in high school kept him out of famous film schools like USC and UCLA, Steven never let that stop him. He was persistent, and it finally paid off. After Universal Studio executives agreed to view one of Spielberg's short films titled *Amblin'*, they were impressed and offered him a seven-year TV directing contract. It was the professional beginning of his phenomenally successful career.

TELL THE NEXT GENERATION DETAIL BY DETAIL THE STORY OF GOD.

PSALM 48:13 MSG

Because of his Jewish roots, Spielberg was always riveted by the effects of the Holocaust and bought the movie rights to the book *Schindler's List*, the true story of a Holocaust survivor, written by Australian author Thomas Keneally, published in 1982. But Spielberg didn't feel ready to make the movie.

In 1993, he said, "Everything I have done up till now has really been a preparation for Schindler. I had to grow into that."

Even his mother wanted him to make the film earlier than he did. She said in an interview, "We of the family kept saying to Steve over the many years, 'When are you going to do *Schindler's List*?' He would just shut us all up with, 'I'm not ready.'"

But when he was ready, his mother, Leah, related, he was ready. He would do it the right way. By this time, Spielberg was a family man married to Kate Capshaw, who had converted to Judaism, and they practiced Jewish traditions in their home. Finally, he was ready to face his own Jewishness and the painful feelings he had experienced as a result of anti-Semitism. Another motivating factor for making the movie was Spielberg's concern that more than 60 percent of high school students had never heard of the Holocaust.

What made the making of this heart-wrenching film bearable for Spielberg was his wife and children, who went to Poland with him, along with his mother Leah and her husband. Many nights he would come home from the set crying because of the emotional intensity and realism of telling the story.

Before *Schindler's List* was released to the public, Spielberg set up a private showing for his mother. "I saw it in an empty theater," Leah is quoted as saying, "just my husband and I. They showed it, and when I came out Steve's secretary was standing in the door with Steve on the phone. He wanted an impression. I was totally mute. I thought I would never speak again."

In March 1994, the film about the Holocaust won an Oscar for Best

Picture, and Spielberg finally won for Best Director.

During the filming of *Schindler's List*, many Holocaust survivors wanted to tell Spielberg their stories so that no one would forget what had happened. After being asked dozens of times, he set up the Survivors of the Shoah Visual History Foundation with the money he earned from his award-winning film. (Shoah in Hebrew means Holocaust.) Thousands of volunteers were trained all over the world to interview and videotape the elderly survivors in their homes, and the project continues to this day. Spielberg is dedicated to preserving these testimonies for as long as there are people to tell their stories.

Because a Jewish mother believed in her son's raw talent, Steven Spielberg became one of the most celebrated and successful filmmakers in history. And her influence has yet another important result. A significant contribution has been made to the education of the next generation concerning Jewish history.

A Mother of Influence is willing to encourage and participate in her child's creative development.

ROSE ELIZABETH FITZGERALD KENNEDY

1890 - 1995

PRESIDENT JOHN FITZGERALD KENNEDY, U.S. SENATORS ROBERT KENNEDY AND EDWARD KENNEDY.

A woman of unshakeable faith, Rose Kennedy infused in her famous

children a strong sense of familial and public duty.

⚬⚬≫⚭≪⚬⚬

S ome historians would say that Rose Kennedy was not a perfect mother, calling her cold, distant, and austere. They point to the fact that as a devout Catholic, she spent much of her time in private prayer in a separate cottage at their Hyannis Port compound, in retreat from her rambunctious children. But in the final analysis, it is a mother's own words and the tributes and accomplishments of her children that speak the loudest.

Rose Kennedy once said, "I looked on child rearing not only as a work of love and duty but as a profession that was fully as interesting and challenging as any honorable profession in the world and one that demanded the best I could bring to it."

Through the years, she actually kept a card file on each of her nine children, tracking their health status. As a wealthy woman, she may never have had to change diapers, but when her famous sons, John F. Kennedy, Robert Kennedy, and Edward Kennedy ran for public office, the fiercely loyal, protective, and ambitious mother was there supporting them in every way possible.

Perhaps some historians are more critical because they fail to under-

MY CHILD . . . DO NOT FORSAKE YOUR MOTHER'S TEACHING.

PROVERBS 6:20 NRSV

stand the era and society in which Rose Kennedy was raised. Even as a teenage girl, she accompanied her father John "Honey Fitz" Fitzgerald, one-time mayor of Boston, to partisan functions—from political rallies to wakes and weddings—and was a young woman of astute political thinking.

She wanted to attend Wellesley College after graduating from high school at the age of sixteen, but instead, her parents sent Rose and her sister Agnes to convent school in the Netherlands. Women were meant to marry and bear children, not seek careers. It was a terribly lonely time for the young girl, but she said that eventually, she "was able to find in herself the place that was meant for God."

Disputing the fact that it was their father more than their mother who raised the nine Kennedy kids, John Kennedy once said, "They talk a lot about Dad. But he was not around all that much. Mother deserves more credit than she gets. She is the one who was there. She is the one who read to us. She took us to Plymouth Rock and the other historic places. She gave me my interest in history."

When her sons were out campaigning, Rose Kennedy was in the thick of it. She always felt that their love of politics was inherited from the Fitzgerald side of the family. "I was giving political speeches before women had the right to vote," she said shortly before her ninetieth birthday. "I have always loved politics."

But her faith was the rudder that steered the political ship. On the morning that her son John was inaugurated as president, she slipped into a pew of a Georgetown church. There she found John praying. "No one, including my son, knew I was there, as I sat in a side pew," she later wrote to a reporter. "I was infinitely pleased and thanked God for the grace which had prompted Jack to start his administration with a prayer on his lips and in his heart."

Along with victory, Rose Kennedy also suffered enormous losses in her lifetime. When President Kennedy was shot, her husband Joe was in ill health at the Hyannis Port compound. Despite her own grief, she gave orders that her husband not be told until the next morning, thinking he would be stronger then. So all the TVs were unplugged, and Rose went for a walk on the beach. In speaking of the tragedy, Rose said, "I can't stand it. I've got to keep moving."

Until her health failed before her death from pneumonia at the age of 104, Rose Kennedy continued to attend daily Mass. It was her faith that sustained her when her sons President John F. Kennedy and Senator Robert Kennedy were killed by assassins' bullets.

At Rose Kennedy's funeral Mass, her son Senator Ted Kennedy said of his mother, "She sustained us in the saddest times—by her faith in God . . . and by the strength of her character, which was a combination of the sweetest gentleness and the most tempered steel."

The influence of this mother born before the turn of the twentieth century not only shaped the lives of her children but also the face of American politics.

A Mother of Influence forges her children's character when they are young.

JACQUELINE MCENTIRE

1919 -

REBA NELL MCENTIRE. A teacher and talented singer,

Jackie McEntire gave her daughter Reba a stable home life

and taught her to sing.

༄

The first song Jackie McEntire taught her daughter Reba to sing was "Jesus Loves Me," and the little girl made her professional debut with it at the age of five in a hotel lobby, earning a big nickel for her efforts.

Born March 28, 1954, and reared on a more than 7,000-acre cattle ranch just outside of Kiowa, Oklahoma, Reba and her brother and sister passed the time singing in the car as they followed their Dad and granddad from rodeo to rodeo. Reba's grandfather was a three-time world champion steer roper, with her dad running close behind. Reba's mother loved to sing, but as a devoted mother, she never pursued her dreams of stardom. Instead, she chose to invest her efforts into providing a loving, stable environment for her children.

The girl who would one day be known as the "Queen of Country Music" learned to harmonize with her sister Susie and brother Pake, performing as the Singing McEntires while they were in school. The siblings even recorded music on the Boss label in 1972, but it was Reba's rendition in 1974 of "The Star-Spangled Banner" at the National Rodeo Finals in Oklahoma City that would capture the attention of a country music star Red Steagall and lead to a recording contract with Mercury Records. Comparing her talent to that of Patsy Cline, Reba has become known as the number one best-selling female artist ever.

Like her mom, Jackie, Reba received a college degree in secondary education and minored in music. Also like her mother, Reba says she is first and foremost a mom, even as she pursues her singing and acting career.

"Being a mother is the greatest gift God has given me," Reba once said in a *Saturday Evening Post* interview. "I cherish it." Speaking of her son, Shelby, the son of second husband Norval Blackstock, her bandleader, she went on to say, "It's hard to share and hard to let him go." But Reba believes it's important that her son have a sense of strong family ties. That's why she regularly sends him off to visit her mom and dad and the rest of her family in Oklahoma.

Family is her life. "My family makes things fun," she said, "and makes me goal-oriented."

Reba also says her mom and dad "set great examples. Daddy gave a lot, although sometimes he wasn't there much. . . . He's hard-working and very driven—I got that from him. My mom was there day to day, all the time. She worked, too, one time even selling fish bait for six dollars a day. We never had a whole lot, but we always had enough. Both my parents taught us to work hard, give 100 percent, and finish your job."

They taught her to laugh, too, and that's one of the qualities she's passing on to her son. "I also want to give him direction, morals, and, I hope, to just follow the Golden Rule."

Reba practices what she preaches, giving selflessly and tirelessly to a number of worthy charities, including The Salvation Army; Texoma Medical Center, which is the home of The Reba McEntire Rehabilitation Center, Reba's Ranch House, and the TMC Reba Mobile Mammography Unit; Children's Medical Research; and Habitat for Humanity. She has been honored by the Salvation Army with a humanitarian award and also supports a variety of other causes, acting as national spokeswoman for First Book, a children's literacy group that provides new books to low-income families. She has also been honored with the Home Depot Humanitarian Award and the Minnie Pearl Humanitarian Award. Her music videos have generated millions of dollars, which Reba has used to help foundations around the world deal with the issues of AIDS and

THE **LORD** IS MY STRENGTH AND MY SHIELD; MY HEART TRUSTS IN HIM, AND I AM HELPED. MY HEART LEAPS FOR JOY AND I WILL GIVE THANKS TO HIM IN SONG.

PSALM 28:7 NIV

abused children.

Reba has a song in her heart because her mother planted it there when she was a little girl and stayed at home where she could nurture its growth. Her influence is evident as her talented daughter shares that song of love with the whole world.

A Mother of Influence provides a loving, stable environment in which her children can grow.

GRACE CORRIGAN

Unknown

CHRISTA CORRIGAN MCAULIFFE. A teacher and

mentor, Grace Corrigan supported her daughter's desire to

be the first teacher in space.

⁕

With a mixture of fear and pride, Grace Corrigan craned her neck upward to watch the Space Shuttle Challenger, carrying her thirty-seven-year-old schoolteacher daughter Christa McAuliffe on her journey into orbit around the earth. The night before the launch, Christa had called her parents to say good-bye.

"She was on a high," her mother Grace said in an interview at the time. "Christa didn't talk about the risks." She had been trained to respond to any number of emergencies aboard the Challenger, but no one had anticipated a catastrophe such as the one that was about to happen.

Seventy-four seconds after liftoff, on January 28, 1986, the space shuttle exploded, shooting debris in all directions like a sparkler as it burns out, and Grace's dreams for her daughter disintegrated and fell to earth.

June Scobee Rodgers, the widow of Challenger commander Francis Scobee said, "The spouses were protected from the public, but Grace wanted to be out with the public when it launched." The nation mourned with her.

But just as Christa would have wanted, her mother carried on with her life and did not succumb to depression. Instead, she became the "keeper of her daughter's flame," according to an article in *People Weekly*. Grace's calendar filled with public appearances across the nation.

"People like to be able to know about Christa," her mother said. "She

[JOSEPH SAID,] "AS FAR AS I AM CONCERNED, GOD TURNED INTO GOOD WHAT YOU MEANT FOR EVIL."

GENESIS 50:20 NLT

touched so many lives."

As a young girl, the oldest child of Edward and Grace Corrigan was fascinated with the Apollo moon-landing program. On Christa's astronaut application, she wrote, "I watched the Space Age being born, and I would like to participate." Her goal to become the first teacher in space was "to humanize the space age by giving a perspective from a non-astronaut."

During her 120 days of training at NASA, Christa also developed a friendly rapport with the news media, and children in classrooms all across America followed her progress. Her intention was to keep a detailed journal about her exploits in space, just as the early pioneers of this country had done, and broadcast lessons from the shuttle. The morning of the explosion, millions of school children watched with great expectation and then with horror as their favorite teacher perished.

But out of the evil of such a senseless accident came great good. The excitement Christa McAuliffe generated about the space program continues to burn in the hearts of young people, and they continue to dream of a future career in space. Elementary schools from California to Florida changed their names to honor her sacrifice.

President Ronald Reagan, during a 1984 speech suggested putting a teacher into space. He spoke directly to schoolchildren after the Challenger disaster. He told them, "I know it's hard to understand, but sometimes things like this happen. It's all part of the process of exploration and discovery. It's all part of taking a chance and expanding man's horizons. The future doesn't belong to the faint-hearted. It belongs to the brave."

Today, with the help of her mother Grace, Christa McAuliffe's legacy continues in the lives of Christa's children, Scott and Caroline, as well as in all the others she touched on that brilliant sunny day in the winter of 1986.

A Mother of Influence helps her children reach for the stars.

Jenna Hawkins Welch

1919 -

Laura Welch Bush. Jenna Welch read

to her daughter each night, and by doing so, passed on

her own passion for books that has contributed to

Laura's continued campaign for literacy.

⬥

"From the time she could open her eyes," Jenna Welch once responded to an interviewer's question about when she began reading to her daughter, Laura. The child who would one day grow up to be First Lady would cuddle with her mother and listen to wonderful stories that sparked her imagination. It was a stable and deeply loving home. Although her parents wanted to have other children, Laura Bush would grow up as an only child.

Perhaps that's why the little girl would line up her dolls in chairs and lecture them like the teacher she would one day become. Since she had no younger brothers or sisters, her dolls became the ones she read to—just as her mother read to her.

Laura's father, Harold, was a successful homebuilder in Midland, Texas, during the oil boom, while her mother worked as the bookkeeper for the business. The First Methodist Church of Midland was their second home. Both Jenna and Harold Welch were devout Methodists and raised Laura in the church, where she sang in the choir from the second grade through high school. Laura's faith has always been a strong force in her life. Later, she and George W. Bush exchanged marriage vows at First

Methodist, and when their twin daughters Jenna and Barbara (named for their grandmothers) were born, they were baptized in that same church.

Jenna Welch and her husband encouraged Laura from an early age to do well in school. Although neither of them finished college, they let her know that they expected her to attain higher education. Never wanting to upset her parents in any way, she became an excellent student and stayed out of trouble.

Laura went on to attend college at Southern Methodist University in Dallas, Texas, where she earned her Bachelor of Science in Education degree in 1968. She taught elementary school until 1972 when she decided to enroll at the University of Texas at Austin. She earned a Master of Library Science degree in 1973. Laura worked as a librarian until she met George W. Bush at the home of mutual friends in 1977. They were married after only a few months in November 1977.

Mrs. Bush became a mother of twin girls in 1981 and an active role model for them as her mother had been for her, emphasizing daily reading and higher education as a goal for the future.

George Bush decided to campaign for the office of Governor of Texas, and Laura became First Lady of that state in 1995. During that time she launched an early childhood development initiative to help parents and caregivers prepare infants and young children for learning and reading when they enter school. She helped write legislation to make that program a reality statewide. The First Lady also kicked off the Texas Book Festival to raise money for the state's public libraries and was involved in raising breast cancer awareness.

During George Bush's run for the presidency in 2000, Laura became an eloquent spokesperson for education topics and has continued that role throughout her husband's tenure as president. However, she never intended to take a front-and-center role as First Lady. That all changed on the morning of September 11, 2001, when terrorists crashed jetliners into the twin towers of the World Trade Center, the Pentagon, and in a Pennsylvania field. The plans for that final plane were thwarted. Its original target was possibly either the White House or the U.S. Capitol, where Laura Bush was preparing to speak about early childhood education before Senator Ted Kennedy's committee.

Before she allowed the Secret Service to whisk her away to a secure location, First Lady Laura Bush faced the television cameras to comfort the nation. "Our hearts and prayers go to the victims of terrorism," she said, "and our support goes to the rescue workers."

Ted Kennedy, who lost his brother President John F. Kennedy to an assassin's bullet, in speaking of those moments after learning of the attack on the World Trade Center in New York, said of Laura Bush, "You take the measure of a person at a time like that. She is steady, assured, elegant."

> I WILL INSTRUCT THEE AND TEACH THEE IN THE WAY WHICH THOU SHALT GO: I WILL GUIDE THEE WITH MINE EYE.
>
> PSALM 32:8 KJV

After addressing the news cameras, Laura Bush tried to contact her daughters, but they had already been taken to secure locations. In the meantime, her husband had been rushed to Air Force One. President Bush finally got through to his wife on the phone, and the two assured one another that they were safe.

"She couldn't have been more calm, resolved, almost placid," President Bush said, "which was a very reassuring thing." He told her he would be home soon, but because the Secret Service feared an attack on the president himself, he spent the next eight hours crisscrossing the U.S. in Air Force One.

That night, Laura Bush called her mother to reassure her and to be reassured . . . but also "just for the comfort of her voice." The bond between mother and only daughter is strong.

In the weeks after 9/11, the First Lady would appear on numerous morning talk shows to calm parents' fears. "The tragedy of September 11," she said in a public service announcement, "was meant to cause fear among all Americans, including our children. We can't let that happen."

All over America, she spoke to children and assured them that they were safe. She asked them to draw pictures of that day, allowing them to express their feelings. In a time of great need, First Lady Laura Bush became a calm and healing presence, a mother to the nation that desperately needed reassurance.

Laura Bush is the second First Lady to hold a post-graduate degree, and in November 2001, she became the first person other than a president to deliver the weekly presidential radio address. She used that time to speak out on the plight of women and children under the oppression of the Taliban regime in Afghanistan.

Laura Welch Bush never set out to have a role in politics; just as she never planned to become First Lady of the United States. She never aspired to it and certainly never foresaw it in her dreams for the future when she was growing up in the small town of Midland, Texas. However, she has adapted to it with relative ease and remarkable energy, in large part because her mother endued her with confidence, values, and a love for reading. What her mother did for her, Laura Bush is now doing for children around the world.

**A Mother of Influence is an active
role model for her children.**

HANNAH LANE BLACKWELL

Unknown

DR. ELIZABETH BLACKWELL. Hannah Blackwell ensured her

daughter Elizabeth, who would become the first woman in America to

obtain a medical degree, the same education as her sons.

⚬≫⚬

W ith her entire family, twelve-year-old Elizabeth Blackwell, the third of nine children, stood expectantly at the railing of the tall sailing ship in 1833, as its canvas sails filled with wind. Behind them was everything familiar and English—in front of them, the perils of a sea voyage and an unknown destiny in New York City. It would be the start of a lifelong learning adventure for the young girl, who was educated—along with her four sisters, as well as her brothers—by private tutors. They had lived a privileged life in England.

Her parents, Hannah and Samuel Blackwell, social activists and highly religious and moral people, were Methodists and vocal dissenters of the Church of England. Despite the family's reluctance, Elizabeth's father felt it was time to pursue economic and religious freedom in America. Her parents firmly believed it was every child's future duty to help reform society. But society stood squarely against them. The prevailing thought in Elizabeth Blackwell's day, expressed by Noah Webster, was that "education is always wrong which raises a woman above the duties of her station." Webster felt women needed only to be "correct in their manners, respectable in their families, and agreeable in society."

A sugar refiner by trade, Elizabeth's father set up another refinery in New York, where he became active in the abolitionist movement. In 1838, the family, looking for financial success, moved again to Cincinnati, Ohio, but misfortune seemed to plague them in the New World. Used to financial security, it was therefore a shock when they lost everything. Samuel Blackwell's death left his wife and children destitute.

Because of the independent way in which they were reared, the children showed remarkable resilience and fortitude. Elizabeth and the other two older girls pitched in to support the family by opening a young ladies' boarding school. They operated it for several years before Elizabeth decided to strike out on her own and accepted a teaching position in Henderson, Kentucky. But her abolitionist sensibilities were challenged by the racial prejudice of the South, and she quit after a year to return to Cincinnati.

Since her mother and father had taught her that a person's life, whether male or female, should be spent in the betterment of society, Elizabeth cast about for an occupation that would tackle an area of moral need. In 1844, a friend and woman who was dying of cancer shared with Elizabeth the embarrassment of being treated by male doctors. She had put off having her symptoms diagnosed because there was no woman doctor to treat her. Because of Elizabeth Blackwell's love of learning, her dying friend urged Elizabeth to pursue medicine.

For years, Elizabeth studied on her own. No medical school would admit a woman, but she continued to knock on their doors. It was only by a fluke—a practical joke voted on by the entire student body of men— that Elizabeth was finally admitted to Geneva Medical College (now Hobart College) in upstate New York. Faculty wives and the women of the nearby town thought she was "either wicked or insane" to pursue medicine, so she kept her nose to the grindstone and graduated at the head of her class in 1849.

Determined to become a surgeon, Dr. Blackwell persuaded the hostile medical community to allow her further study in Philadelphia hospitals. After several months, she traveled to Paris to study with physicians there but was met with hostility because she was a woman. Finally, she was admitted to La Maternite, a midwifery school where she studied obstetrics and learned to care for ill children as well. While caring for a child with a severe eye infection caused by gonorrhea, Elizabeth accidentally squirted some of the pus into her own eye. She contracted ophthalmia neonatorum, a severe form of conjunctivitis, and eventually, her eye had to be removed. Her dreams of being a surgeon were dashed, but that did not stop her from the practice of medicine.

Barred from hospitals in Paris, Elizabeth traveled to London where she studied under Sir James Paget in St. Bartholomew's Hospital. She met Florence Nightingale there, who would later defy society to study nursing.

Returning to the U.S., she found no male physicians willing to allow her to set up practice with them. Her younger sister, Emily, was also trying to become a woman doctor, but having an even harder time finding someone to train her. It did not deter them.

THERE IS NEITHER JEW NOR GREEK, THERE IS NEITHER BOND NOR FREE, THERE IS NEITHER MALE NOR FEMALE: FOR YE ARE ALL ONE IN CHRIST JESUS.

GALATIANS 3:28 KJV

Elizabeth eventually found space in a boardinghouse to treat patients, but the other roomers were so scandalized by a woman doctor, they protested and moved out. She was forced to rent a house, living in the attic while using the rooms below as her office. However, the sick were just as distrustful of women doctors as the medical community. By the summer of 1852, she only had three patients a week.

Dr. Blackwell stiffened her resolve, and within two years she opened the New York Dispensary for Poor Women and Children in a slum on the Lower East Side of Manhattan. It was a slow start, but the women finally came, and Dr. Blackwell's practice had to move to a larger space.

In 1857, after further study in Europe, Dr. Blackwell opened the New York Infirmary for Indigent Women and Children. Her sister Emily had finally received medical training and joined Elizabeth in her work.

As women who had challenged the conventions of the day, the Blackwell sisters hoped to open their own medical school for women, but the Civil War intervened, and they spent their time training nurses. However, in 1868, they finally opened the Women's Medical College of New York, which became highly successful and respected.

Elizabeth specialized in hygiene and lectured extensively about the prevention of disease, advocating better sanitation in all areas of life. In 1869, she returned to her roots in England, founded the National Health Society of London, and helped to establish the London School of Medicine for Women, where she headed up the gynecology department until she became too ill by 1879 to teach any longer.

Although Dr. Elizabeth Blackwell never married or had children of her own, she became a mother when she adopted a seven-year-old Irish girl by the name of Kitty Barry. Kitty would devote her life to her adopt-ed mother and live with her until Elizabeth's death on May 31, 1910, in Hastings, England.

Hannah Blackwell's legacy of the equal pursuit of education for her daughters changed the face of medicine forever. It is because of her devo-tion that today women physicians work side by side with their male col-leagues to break the barriers of science and pioneer new drugs and treat-ments that assist us all.

A Mother of Influence teaches her children to pursue education regardless of the obstacles.

EDNA LYBYER VINCENT

Unknown

LYNNE V. CHENEY. Natrona County, Wyoming, deputy sheriff

Edna Vincent taught her daughter Lynne, now wife of Vice President

Dick Cheney, to be self-reliant.

⟨◈⟩

Lynne Vincent Cheney, now the wife of Vice President Dick Cheney, grew up on the stories her mother, Edna, and grandmothers told about her ancestors. She learned Wyoming women hail from hardy stock-strong, independent pioneer types who fought hard to settle their part of the Wild West. They were tough and fierce when they had to be and worked hard at whatever they did. In fact, in 1869 the state of Wyoming was the first to give women the right to vote and wrote it into its constitution in 1889, some thirty-six years before the U.S. Constitution. Wyoming even elected the first woman governor in 1925.

"I had women in my life who always worked," Lynne Cheney once said in an interview. "It honestly never occurred to me that I wouldn't."

The young Lynne Vincent worked hard, achieving success in every area she tackled. Even though it was the 1950s, when girls were not expected to reach for higher education, it never occurred to Lynne that she couldn't fulfill her ambitions just because she was a girl. After all, Mom was a deputy sheriff, and as Lynne Cheney wrote in her book *A is for Abigail: An Almanac of Amazing American Women*, one of seven she has authored, her great-great-grandmother Fannie Peck, a plucky seven-year-old, had walked barefoot beside a covered wagon to save her shoes for

Sunday wear as the family followed the Mormon trail to Utah.

Growing up on the stories told by her mother and grandmothers about her pioneering ancestors, Lynne Cheney developed a great love for history and believes that schools need to do a better job of connecting the human dimension of history to facts and dates. She has spent much of her adult life writing and speaking about the importance of sparking a desire to know our American heritage.

Lynne began dating Dick Cheney in 1957 at Natrona County High School in Caspar, Wyoming. She was the homecoming queen and an outstanding student; he was the football team cocaptain and good enough academically to win a Yale scholarship.

She raced through graduate school, and in 1970 after receiving a Ph.D., she realized there was a glut of academics in the job market and that a pure academic career might be out of reach. So she turned to writing for more general markets.

While her husband, Dick, acted as President Gerald Ford's chief of staff, served six terms as a congressman from Wyoming, was appointed President George H. W. Bush's Secretary of Defense, entered the private sector to work for oil corporation Halliburton and then was named as George W. Bush's running mate, his wife Lynne wasn't sitting around twiddling her thumbs. Lynne Cheney taught college English (she holds a doctorate in nineteenth century British literature), served as a magazine editor, wrote several fiction and nonfiction books, cohosted CNN's "Crossfire Sunday," and served two terms as chair of the National Endowment for the Humanities during the Reagan Administration. She continues to write and serve the American Enterprise Institute as Second Lady.

During the time she served as chairman of the National Endowment for the Humanities—1986 to 1993—she published a report titled "American Memory," which talks about the failure of schools to transfer the knowledge of our past to the generations of the future.

"A system of education that fails to nurture memory of the past denies its students a great deal," she wrote in the report: "the satisfactions of mature thought, an attachment to abiding concerns, a perspective on human existence." She fervently believes that we must teach our children that freedom is not inevitable. It is a renewable commodity that must be won over and again. "This realization," she said, "should make the liberty we enjoy all the more important to us, all the worth defending."

In speaking of her children's alphabet book titled *America: A Patriotic Primer*, illustrated by Robin Preiss Glasser, Lynne Cheney said, "Robin and I started working on this book before the tragic events of September 11. For both of us, it is now more important than ever that our children and grandchildren know the foundation of American freedom and understand why we hold this nation dear." In the introduction to the book, Mrs. Cheney said, "I wrote this book because I want my grandchildren to understand how blessed we are." To underscore her motives, she has donated all of her net proceeds from the book to the American Red Cross and other groups across the country that teach an appreciation of American history, such as the National Center for the American Revolution at Valley Forge.

HER CHILDREN STAND AND BLESS HER. HER HUSBAND PRAISES HER: "THERE ARE MANY VIRTUOUS AND CAPABLE WOMEN IN THE WORLD, BUT YOU SURPASS THEM ALL!"

PROVERBS 31:28-29 NLT

After the terrorist attack of September 11, 2001, Lynne Cheney became "even more passionate about instilling in American youth an appreciation of the values that underpin democracy," according to Los Angeles Times reporter Richard Lee Colvin. In her children's book, the letter "G" stands for God. It may not be a politically correct choice, but Mrs. Cheney believes that it's appropriate to speak of our faith now. Since September 11, "people have become more serious and more willing to talk about deep topics like religion," she said to Washington Times interviewer Jen Waters. "There have been eloquent commentators who have talked about how we have pushed religion out of the public square. I think it is a good thing to have God back in."

Lynne Cheney continues to pass on the stories passed down to her by her mother to her own two daughters and three granddaughters. She believes it's important for them to not only know their history but also to be involved in competitive sports, something that she could not do as a young girl. She did the next best thing then —she became a champion baton twirler and an outstanding scholar.

"I think the move today toward women's athletics has been terrific," she said in an interview with The American Enterprise Institute for Public Policy Research. "Both our daughters are good athletes. Elizabeth, our older daughter, is a terrific downhill skier. Mary is a wonderful snow-boarder and plays ice hockey. Sports are good for women because it teaches you how to play hurt. Women sometimes think if you get knocked down, either literally or figuratively, you go into your room and cry. But what you learn in sports is that if you get knocked down, get back up and try to get that ball in the net the next time."

Lynne Cheney has said Wyoming will always be home. Her roots are there—the roots watered by stories Edna Cheney told when she was a child, stories that strongly influenced who she is today.

A Mother of Influence tells her children the family stories.

NELLE WILSON REAGAN

1883-1962

RONALD WILSON REAGAN. By participating in church activities
with her son, Nelle instilled in Ronald the ideals of God and the Bible
in everyday life, which he carried with him into the
White House as President of the United States.

❦

O ne cold, winter evening, a man staggered down the front walk,
stumbled up the steps, and collapsed on the porch, his dark hair
wet with melting snow. Jack Reagan, normally a congenial, loving, and likable man, was drunk after returning home from another long
night of drinking.

Since Jack couldn't walk without falling down, it was up to his son
Ronnie to help his drunken father into the house. Struggling to the bedroom weighted down by his dad, Ronnie finally managed to put him to
bed. Feeling anger, resentment, yet pity, Ronald Reagan sought out his
mother, Nelle, to vent. She explained to her son the effect alcohol had on
his father and that it was an illness that only Jack could overcome. She
helped Ronnie see that he did not "own" the problem or its consequences
and that he needed to get on with his life. Her words would be repeated
many times over the years ahead.

Perhaps to escape her husband's alcoholism, Nelle was instrumental
in involving the family in the religious revivals of the time. A soft-spoken
woman, she donated much of her time and whatever money she could
spare to charity. She was a leader of church life in her community and
included Ronnie as an actor in the religious skits she supervised. As a
young man, Ronald Reagan led the Easter sunrise services and cleaned

and worked at the church. Due to his mother's guidance during those formative years, Ronald's acting skills and religious beliefs were fused together and would remain with him throughout his life.

Despite Jack's drinking problem, the Reagan family was a happy one, even though, as Ronald once said, "We were poor, but we didn't know we were poor." They moved from town to town and from house to house seeking a place for Jack Reagan to earn a living. This was the time of the Great Depression when many families lived the same lifestyle.

After high school, Ronald Reagan attended Eureka College from 1928 to 1932. During this time he developed a skill for last-minute memorization that was, in the words of his brother Neil, "photographic." It was this skill that would serve him well as an actor. Upon graduation he became a radio sports announcer, and success in that field led to a movie screen test in 1937 and a contract in film. Over the next twenty years, Reagan became famous for his cool vocal command and grace under pressure as he acted in numerous movies and on television.

During his tenure as president of the Screen Actors Guild, Reagan's disputes with other professionals over the issue of communism shifted his political views from liberal to conservative. He was making a name for himself in the political arena, and in 1966 he was elected as the Republican Governor of California, holding that office until 1974.

In a speech given in Dallas in 1980, shortly after accepting the Republican nomination for President, Ronald Reagan reflected the values he had learned from his mother, declaring that if he were shipwrecked and could choose only one book to read for the rest of his life, he would choose the Bible. He went on to say that "all the complex questions facing us at home and abroad have their answer in that single book." He won the presidential nomination in 1981 and served two terms.

After an assassination attempt on President Reagan's life in March 1981, he spoke of his mother's wisdom in a letter: "I found myself remembering that my mother's strongest belief was that all things happen for a reason. She would say, 'We may not understand the why of such things, but if we accept them and go forward, we find, down the road a ways, there was a reason and that everything happens for the best.' Her greatest gift to me was an abiding and unshakable faith in God."

Ronald Reagan carried his mother's insight into the presidency with him and would often refer to the core faith he inherited from her. In a White House ceremony on May 6, 1982, he shared, "I've said before that the most sublime picture in American history is of George Washington on his knees in the snow at Valley Forge. That image personifies a people who know that it's not enough to depend on our own courage and goodness; we must also seek help from God, our Father and Preserver."

Later, in January 1984, he said, "Let's begin at the beginning. God is the center of our lives; the human family stands at the center of society; and our greatest hope for the future is in the faces of our children."

There are many things that a person never remembers from childhood. He rarely remembers every scraped knee, every reprimand, or every home-cooked meal. What a person tends to remember are the character traits of a parent—fairness, consistency, love. As Ronald Reagan observed his mother, Nelle, in everyday life, he saw that she made prayer a daily habit. He may not have remembered each and every one of her prayers, but he did remember that she was a person of prayer. Her example of faith led him through a lifetime of decisions.

Nelle Wilson Reagan would never know how far her son would go with her teachings. She didn't live to see him become Governor of California, or President of the United States, or hear his Berlin speech in which he said, "Mr. Gorbachev, tear down that Wall!" or be a witness to the decisions he made which helped end the Cold War with the Soviet Union. However, because she was a positive role model for him in his youth, Ronald Reagan achieved his highest dreams and influenced the world.

> I AM PERSUADED, THAT NEITHER DEATH, NOR LIFE, NOR ANGELS, NOR PRINCIPALITIES, NOR POWERS, NOR THINGS PRESENT, NOR THINGS TO COME . . . SHALL BE ABLE TO SEPARATE US FROM THE LOVE OF GOD, WHICH IS IN CHRIST JESUS OUR LORD.
>
> ROMANS 8:38-39 KJV

A Mother of Influence knows that her children are likely to live up to what she believes of them.

Betsy Holton Moody

1804 - 1895

DWIGHT LYMAN MOODY. Betsy Moody's perseverance of character was an example to her son D.L. Moody, who would become a world-famous evangelist.

When a friend of D. L. Moody first met his mother, Betsy, he exclaimed, "I see now where you got your vim and hard sense." And it was true, the mother's determination and enthusiasm for life was evident in her son's life. She built a fierceness for right and wrong into her seven boys. One morning she took all of them to the altar of her church and made them swear vengeance on whiskey and everything that was an enemy to the human family.

Life was not easy for the Moody household. Dwight's father died bankrupt and left Betsy with not only seven boys, but two girls as well—nine children—to raise. Creditors came and took everything the family had, even down to the wood and kindling. One morning the house was so cold, the children stayed in bed to keep warm. Lying in their beds, they heard chopping outside. An uncle had come and was cutting the biggest load of firewood the family had ever seen!

For Betsy, there was nothing to do but press on. She milked the family's cows; she spun yarn, wove it into cloth, and made the family's clothes. She cooked, she cleaned, and she juggled their meager finances. And she did it all with a smile. But late at night after all the children were in bed, she would cry until she fell asleep exhausted.

Betsy Moody was of Puritan ancestry, but later in life became a staunch Unitarian. While still a child, Dwight L. Moody was baptized into the Unitarian church.

Without fail, every day Betsy taught her children a Bible lesson, and every Sunday they went to church.

Betsy did not approve when her son Dwight experienced a conversion experience under the guidance of his Sunday school teacher. Neither was she proud or excited when he gathered children together to form a Sunday school class that eventually numbered more than 1,500 students. And she refused to hear him preach when he became an evangelist of great effectiveness. Nor was she among those who rejoiced when he and his friend Ira Sankey spent two years in England, Scotland, and Ireland preaching the Gospel.

> CREATE IN ME A CLEAN HEART, O GOD; AND RENEW A RIGHT SPIRIT WITHIN ME. CAST ME NOT AWAY FROM THY PRESENCE; AND TAKE NOT THY HOLY SPIRIT FROM ME. RESTORE UNTO ME THE JOY OF THY SALVATION; AND UPHOLD ME WITH THY FREE SPIRIT.
>
> PSALM 51:10-12 KJV

But in 1875 D.L. Moody returned from one of his successful London campaigns to his home in Northfield, Connecticut, to preach. The family still lived on the old farm and still went to Sunday meetings in the farm wagon just as they had always done. On one Sunday morning the family was getting ready to drive to town to hear Dwight preach. Betsy turned to her daughter and said, "I don't suppose there would be room in the wagon for me this morning, would there?"

Since she was a Unitarian, no one had thought she would ever be interested in going to church with them. There was plenty of room for the mother of the well-known evangelist! That morning Moody preached with fervor from Psalm 51. At the end of the sermon, he asked those who wanted prayer to stand, and lo and behold, his mother stood to her feet. The overwhelmed evangelist turned to another preacher and said with great emotion, "You pray, Jacobs, I can't."

That was the turning point for Betsy, and she became her son's strongest ally in his war against sin and evil. She was a wise woman. D.L. Moody once said, "Whenever I wanted real sound counsel, I used to go to my mother." And no matter where the great evangelist traveled, his steps always led him back to her. Moody would slip away regularly to the Northfield hills, where his mother sat with her thoughts upon him and his work, praising God who had permitted her boy to become the instrument of so much blessing.

In her later years Betsy Moody could not travel much, so her son brought speakers and singers to her. On one occasion he brought a group of young men who were part of a student conference to her home. He told them, "My mother is too feeble to attend our meetings. She is deeply interested in this work, and she has prayed earnestly for its success. I want her to hear some of you speak and sing. I want you to receive my mother's blessing before we go to the mountains to pray, for next to the blessing of God, I place that of my mother."

When at last Betsy shook off her human body at age 91, her son summed up what her life had meant to him in a few short words. "I think she has been the best mother in the world," he said. "She was one of the noblest characters this world has ever seen. She was as true as sunlight; I never knew that woman to deceive me."

A Mother of Influence teaches her children to seek the truth.

Juliette Gordon Low

1860-1927

The Girl Scouts of America. Juliette "Daisy" Low founded an organization that has for generations helped girls learn to make good choices and improve their lives.

⤜✖⤏

As a young woman, Georgia-born "Daisy" spent much of her time giving or attending parties and flitting from one pet project to another. She was charming and entertaining, but those who weren't her friends often thought of her as odd and undependable. She had health problems, could barely hear, and had no children.

But then, at age forty-six, Daisy found herself a restless, lonely widow. She longed to do something worthwhile, even as she slowly returned to her life of parties and travel. Then in May 1911, six years after her husband died, Daisy met the famous British war hero General Sir Robert Baden-Powell at a luncheon. He was the founder of the Boy Scouts, and what Sir Robert told Daisy about his work fascinated her.

In March of the next year, she formed two "Girl Guide" patrols. Each girl was given a notebook, pencil, and a yard of cord to practice knot typing. The first name to ever appear under the "Promise" was Daisy's niece and namesake, Margaret "Daisy Doots" Gordon.

By the time the first handbook was published in 1913, the organization's name had officially become "Girl Scouts." Two years later, the

DON'T HIDE YOUR
LIGHT! LET IT
SHINE FOR ALL;
LET YOUR GOOD
DEEDS GLOW FOR
ALL TO SEE, SO
THAT THEY WILL
PRAISE YOUR
HEAVENLY FATHER.

MATTHEW 5:15-16 TLB

first national convention was held, and the following year, a group to serve younger girls—called the Brownies—was organized. Daisy, who had no children of her own, was making a big difference in the lives of thousands of America's daughters.

From the beginning, Daisy sought to give girls more value in their lives, and in turn, she valued the girls in her life. Her first troop outside her home in Scotland was mostly of poor girls who were facing the prospect of leaving home at an early age to work as maids in the city. Daisy developed troop projects to help them earn money raising chickens and spinning wool, which enabled them to stay home with their families. Whenever a problem arose in the Girl Scouts, Daisy's first response was, "Ask the girls. They'll know what's best." This was a radical approach at the time, when few thought children had the ability to make choices.

The Girl Guides took over all of Daisy's thoughts and energy. She paid the organization's expenses the first four years and traveled widely to help interested persons organize new troops. She called on Mrs. Woodrow Wilson, the president's wife, to be the honorary president of the Girl Scouts. Mrs. Wilson accepted, and each subsequent First Lady has been the honorary president of the Girl Scouts.

With increasing numbers of troops, and thus increasing costs, Daisy became the organization's principal fund-raiser. For this task, she called upon her lifelong eccentricity and playfulness. When friends declined her invitation to donate funds or work for the Girl Scouts, she would play on her deafness by pretending she could not hear them. One of her favorite ploys was to wear a hat trimmed with parsley and carrots to fashionable luncheons. When asked about her hat, she would say, "I can't afford to have this hat done over. I have to save my money for my Girl Scouts. You know about the Girl Scouts, don't you?" When she died, there were nearly 168,000 members of the Girl Scouts. Today, there are more than 3.4 million.

A less vibrant personality might have become a recluse because of her hearing loss, but not Daisy. Her passion for living and eternal optimism placed her in a position to be a positive influence on the lives of many generations of young girls.

A Mother of Influence expects the best from her children and encourages them to make good choices for themselves.

MORROW COFFEY GRAHAM

1892 - 1981

WILLIAM (BILLY) FRANKLIN GRAHAM. Morrow Coffey

Graham prayed for her son Billy, who would become a world-renowned

evangelist, and taught him to trust God and believe the Bible.

⟨∞⟩

O n the day Billy was born, Morrow Coffey Graham spent much
of the afternoon picking beans and standing at the kitchen sink
getting them ready for canning. Soon those beans would be
added to the rows of canned fruits and vegetables shelved, ready, and
waiting for the winter months—a harvest of plenty. She was a dairy
farmer's wife in North Carolina and used to hard work. There was always
too much to do in helping to run the farm—milking, canning, gardening,
and so much more.

Morrow never earned university degrees or made great speeches or
wrote books. This mother of one of the world's greatest evangelists simply
knew how to pray, and pray she did.

"I pray without ceasing for Billy," she said once in an interview with
Christianity Today. "The resources of the Christian mother are limited
solely by the love and grace of God. It is to Him that she turns in prayer,
not only for the strength needed for each day but also for blessings for
her children. Through prayer there comes wisdom, understanding, and
grace. As our children sense our prayer lives they too learn the vital place
of communion with our Heavenly Father."

The Graham family had four children, the oldest of them Billy.
Morrow and her husband, William, were strict Calvinists who showed

their son that hard work and honesty were the way all people should live in God's world. This country-bred and country-raised woman with a shy smile instilled in her son a love for the Bible. Even when he showed no interest, she continued to share truths from God's Word until at last they penetrated his heart and the phrase "the Bible says" became his hallmark.

Morrow and William were married for forty-six years when God called William home. While she missed him dreadfully, she did not mope or engage in useless activity. Instead, she devoted herself more than ever to prayer — prayer for Billy, prayer for all her children, their spouses, and all her grandchildren and great-grandchildren.

Words of wisdom about living a life of faith poured continually from her mouth. Once when it looked as though her leg would have to be amputated, she endured the pain until at last the infection subsided and she was sent home from the hospital. She said, "God doesn't comfort us to make us comfortable, but to make us comforters."

> WE HAVE NOT CEASED TO PRAY FOR YOU AND TO ASK THAT YOU MAY BE FILLED WITH THE KNOWLEDGE OF HIS WILL IN ALL SPIRITUAL WISDOM AND UNDERSTANDING, SO THAT YOU MAY WALK IN A MANNER WORTHY OF THE LORD, TO PLEASE HIM IN ALL RESPECTS, BEARING FRUIT IN EVERY GOOD WORK AND INCREASING IN THE KNOWLEDGE OF GOD.
>
> COLOSSIANS 1:9-10 NASB

Morrow Graham could quote and remember scriptures and apply them to everyday living with ease. Untrained by a theological seminary, she kept putting together the bits of truths she learned from her daily Bible study and in the end became a woman whose biblical knowledge touched untold numbers of people.

Even at the end of her life, when multiple strokes had taken their toll and she needed a full-time caregiver, Morrow reasoned that God had not yet taken her home because there was more prayer work to be done. When it came to her attention that there was a need in someone's life, she would pray, but that's not all. She also would ask her caregiver to write a note of comfort and put a few dollars in the envelope to help out. It was her way.

One day, while Billy Graham was on a revival campaign in France, he called her at home. Weak and in pain, she passed on through her caregiver a verse for her preacher son: "For this cause we also, since the day we heard it, do not cease to pray for you, and to desire that ye might be filled with the knowledge of his will in all wisdom and spiritual understanding" (Colossians 1:9 KJV).

What a legacy! What grace from a dying woman, to bless her son one more time with the confirmation of her prayers! Just a few weeks later Morrow went home to be with her Lord. But her legacy lives on in her children and their children and their children's children.

This steadfast woman of God trained and gave the world her son who has perhaps preached to more people than anyone who has ever lived on earth. He has counseled and prayed with presidents. He has held more than 400 crusades in 185 countries. He has won a Congressional Gold Medal and the Ronald Reagan Presidential Foundation Freedom Award, among many others. But most of all, he has lived a consistent life of single focus: that of sharing the good news of the Gospel.

A Mother of Influence prays diligently for her children.

NANCY HANKS LINCOLN

1784-1818

SARA BUSH JOHNSTON LINCOLN

1788-1869

ABRAHAM LINCOLN'S mother and stepmother encouraged the
future President of the United States to read and aspire to a greater life
than farming, even when others thought him lazy.

⟨∞⟩

As Nancy Hanks Lincoln, born to a well-bred farmer in West
Virginia, trekked westward with her family, finally pushing
through the Cumberland Gap into the frontier of Kentucky, she
often talked with other travelers she met on the way about what lay ahead
of them.

Lots of families were moving west in search of better opportunities.
They traveled in ox carts or walked beside one-seater buggies piled high
with their belongings. Others rode on horseback on the narrow trails or
pushed wheelbarrows full of baggage. It wasn't an easy journey.

Settled in Kentucky, Nancy became skilled in needlework and was an
excellent seamstress. As such she was hired to sew everything from wedding gowns to funeral attire. She became known for her work ethic, neat-
ness, cheerfulness, and intelligence, and she was deeply religious.

It was in Kentucky that she met and married Thomas Lincoln. A year
later a little girl, Sarah, was born to the couple. And two years later on
February 12, 1809, Nancy delivered a healthy baby boy one stormy

morning as she lay on a bed of poles covered with corn husks in a one-room cabin near Hodgenville, Kentucky. Abraham Lincoln was named after his grandfather.

After a while Nancy, Thomas, and their children moved to southern Indiana. Life went along quite well for a while. Nancy was a good and loving mother, who often read to her children from the family's Bible. She was ambitious for them and hoped they would have opportunities in life that she and Thomas had missed.

Then in 1818 tragedy struck the Lincoln family. Milk fever attacked the town of Little Pigeon Creek where they lived. Milk fever is a disease contracted by drinking milk from cows that have grazed on poisonous white snakeroot. Nancy took ill, and for a week she struggled to get better, but then realized she would not live. Before her death, she called her children to her bedside and asked them to be good and kind to their father, to each other, and to the world, and then she died. Nine-year-old Abraham helped his father carve the pegs for her coffin. Everything this woman was to her son can be summed up in his words. "I remember my mother's prayers and they have always followed me," Abraham Lincoln once said. "They have clung to me all my life. God bless my mother; all that I am or ever hope to be, I owe to her."

Another year passed and the widower Thomas took another bride: Sara Bush Johnston. This loving stepmother discovered that her new stepson was very intelligent and had a passion for knowledge. She inspired the ambitious but unschooled boy to discipline and educate himself.

"Abe read all the books he could lay his hands on—and when he came upon a passage that struck him, he would write it down on boards if he had not paper and keep it there till he did get paper," Sara said of her stepson. Although she could not read or write herself, she once gave him three books. In that day books were considered a priceless treasure because they were so scarce on the frontier. It was a wonderful and treasured gift. Stepmother and stepson developed a close, intimate, mother-son relationship that continued for the rest of Abraham Lincoln's life.

Sara was proud of her stepson and at times probably stood between the boy and his father who felt that Abraham spent too much time reading and studying. While on one hand Thomas wanted his son to be educated in a way he had not been, on the other hand he felt young Abe should be working and not reading. An uncle said that Abe's father "slashed" at him for neglecting his work. Others too saw Abe as sometimes "lazy" when he neglected his work in order to read. One man said, "Abe was awful lazy: he worked for me and was always reading and thinking. I used to get mad at him."

Sara knew Abe didn't like physical labor. Laziness was regarded as something between a character fault and a cardinal sin. But while his adoring stepmother saw the laziness, she saw something else too. She saw that the young man was industrious toward knowledge. This was the way in which he could assert his individuality and aspirations. And aspire, he did. He began climbing the long slow ladder of success that would eventually make him the sixteenth president of the United States.

ENCOURAGE THOSE WHO ARE TIMID. TAKE TENDER CARE OF THOSE WHO ARE WEAK. BE PATIENT WITH EVERYONE.

1 THESSALONIANS 5:14 NLT

As an adult Abraham Lincoln remained close to his stepmother, whom he always referred to as "Mother." Even after he had gone out on his own, he kept a forty-acre plot of land in his name "for Mother while she lives." He'd visit her every year or two and saw to it as best he could that she was well cared for.

After Abraham Lincoln was elected to the presidency in 1860, he made one more visit to see his stepmother before he left for Washington. Together they went to visit the grave of his father, Thomas, who had died in 1851. It was as though Sara had a premonition she would never see her beloved stepson again. And she never did. He died in Ford's Theater at the hands of an assassin four years before Sara herself passed away.

Abraham Lincoln was truly blessed to have had two mothers who loved him deeply. Together, these two women shaped the life of one of the best-loved men the world has ever known.

A Mother of Influence encourages her children to seek knowledge.

PAULINE EINSTEIN

1858 - 1919

ALBERT EINSTEIN. Pauline Einstein believed in her son Albert's

abilities, even when his school branded him as a slow learner.

᎖᎖᎖

Pauline Einstein, a good Jewish woman, was concerned when her son Albert passed his third birthday and was still not talking. Was he normal? She breathed a sigh of relief when he at last began to speak.

But her fears increased when he entered school. Albert was considered a slow learner; some of his teachers thought he might even be disabled. Pauline watched and worried as he struggled through almost every class. The boy could not read well, spelling defeated him, and it seemed impossible for him to memorize his multiplication tables. Only by faith could Pauline hold on to her belief that her son Albert would succeed in life.

No one in those days understood Albert's problems—the boy was extremely intelligent and also severely dyslexic. Yet his curiosity drove him to think about problems and their solutions and pay attention to things he did not understand. A favorite toy was a compass his father had given him. Unwilling to just play with the toy, he insisted on finding out how it worked. What force set the needle of the compass swinging?

German schools of the time had strict disciplinary policies. Albert rebelled, and eventually he was expelled. But that did not stop his quest for knowledge. He began to teach himself, beginning with religion. First, he avidly studied the Bible. Then he turned to science and math and became totally absorbed in these subjects.

As Pauline observed Albert's struggle, it seemed to her that her son's problem was a lack of focus. Since she was an accomplished pianist, she understood the discipline needed to learn to play an instrument and thought it might help him concentrate better. Perhaps if she shared with him her love of music by having him master the violin, he could learn something about being attentive long enough to grasp information. He was only five years old when she put the instrument in his hands. He was decidedly not interested. He did not want to play the violin, and most of all he did not want to practice and said so with great vehemence. Pauline paid no attention to his protests and forced him to continue. Many years later he would thank her. Playing the violin became one of his favorite ways to relax.

> **FAITH IS THE SUB-STANCE OF THINGS HOPED FOR, THE EVIDENCE OF THINGS NOT SEEN.**
>
> HEBREWS 11:1 KJV

Pauline watched Albert's interest in science, and it was she who encouraged him most. Her husband, Herman, was occupied with the building and losing of a couple of businesses. When Albert Einstein was only fifteen, his father's business failed again, and the family relocated to Milan, Italy. Albert stayed behind in Switzerland to attend school, and his parents continued to support his scientific interests, such as the work on his theory of $E=mc^2$. After about a year of being on his own Albert left school and rejoined his family in Milan. Not long after, his father, Herman, died. It was a great blow to the young man. The immediate future was filled with frustration and discouragement.

Upon graduation, Albert could find no teaching positions, so he settled for a job tutoring and performing calculations. He sent his one published work out to numerous professors seeking to find a job, but his efforts yielded no employment. At last a friend came to his aid, and he was recommended for a position in the Bern Patent Office. It was a perfect solution for him. The position gave him time to continue his research and calculations while being employed. While he waited for his patent office job to begin, he wrote a research paper on thermodynamics that was published. He then attempted to have it accepted as a Ph.D. thesis. That didn't work either.

Eventually things began to come together for the young Albert Einstein, and he was given a full professorship at the German University in Prague. Only a year later he was given another position as Professor of Theoretical Physics in Zurich. Best of all, he was allowed to do all the research he wanted at the university. Two more years passed, and he became the Director and Professor of Theoretical Physics at the University of Berlin. Others had finally recognized his talents and superior intellect.

When his mother, Pauline, died in 1919, it was a great shock to Albert, and he felt her loss deeply. It was she who had believed in him when others wrote him off. It was she who had literally forced him to study the violin and helped his dyslexic brain learn to focus. It was she who had supported his scientific endeavors and believed in him even when no one else did.

Maybe Einstein summed up his life and the contribution his mother had made when he said, "There are only two ways to live your life. One is as though nothing is a miracle. The other is as though everything is a miracle." Albert Einstein was Pauline's miracle, and she believed in him no matter what others said.

A Mother of Influence believes in her children.

PLEASANT ROWLAND

1941 -

AMERICAN GIRLS. Successful businesswoman Pleasant Rowland

gave young girls of America historical role models when she created the

books and dolls of the American Girls line.

⟡

A trip to Colonial Williamsburg in Virginia gave birth to the idea that Pleasant Rowland would turn into the American Girls Collection of books, dolls, and accessories.

"I was tired of the cheap-looking merchandise being pitched at children through Saturday morning cartoons, and seeing book spin-offs from those," Pleasant told Publishers Weekly in an interview. "It seemed backward to me."

Pleasant Rowland loved history, and she banked everything on an idea that girls 7-12 years old would love to read touching, adventurous stories about girls just like themselves who had lived in earlier times.

In 1986, using $1 million of her own money, bank loans, and investment capital, Pleasant launched a direct market business for her collection, despite the skepticism of her own friends and family. No one thought she could succeed in a world already populated with Barbie dolls. But she had a dream and an ambition to "show how some things change and other things stay the same." She bet on the intelligence of American girls and that their imaginations would be ignited by the accomplishments of women throughout history. The rest, as they say, is history.

For the first three dolls, Pleasant invented them and their backgrounds: Circa 1854 Kirsten, a Swedish immigrant to the American frontier; Victorian orphan Samantha, living with her grandmother in 1904; and Molly McIntire, who lived through World War II. Pleasant hired authors Valerie Tripp and Janet Shaw to bring the girls to life in their books, and she found first-rate artists to render the illustrations. Then she contracted with a German doll-maker to create the dolls. Pleasant insisted on accuracy, and every product had to meet her exacting standards.

Not wanting to waste her advertising money, Pleasant believed direct mail would be the best way to reach the girls who would be interested in the American Girls Collection. Despite dire predictions, she assembled a mailing list of about half a million names, mailed beautiful four-color catalogs, installed three telephone order lines, and waited for the results. They were more than she could have imagined! Within a few short months, Pleasant's company had sold more than $1.8 million worth of merchandise, and by 1990, sales reached more than $50 million! In 2003, the company was worth more than $350 million.

What made the Pleasant Company and the American Girls collection so successful? Pleasant Rowland's values and attention to detail.

"I think it's very hard for people to raise children today," Pleasant told a Madison, Wisconsin magazine writer. "There's not a lot of support from the world at large for people who are trying to instill solid values in their children. And they are working against a tide of cheap, transient mass culture, most of which is really tawdry and damaging to the moral fiber of this country. I think we stand against that. We are a little beacon of light and a ray of hope for parents who are trying to do the right thing by their children."

Because of her company's great success, she was approached in 1998 by Mattel, Inc. to purchase the American Girl brand, and after much soul-searching, Pleasant felt the giant corporation could increase the collection's awareness around the world. However, she remained at the helm of American Girls as vice chairman of Mattel until her retirement in July of 2000.

With such entrepreneurial success you would expect that Pleasant Rowland must have an M.B.A. or must have been a top executive in a toy company. Not so. Prior to founding the Pleasant Company in 1985, Pleasant graduated from Wells College in 1962, worked as an elementary teacher and as a news reporter and anchor for KGO-TV in San Francisco, and served as vice president of Boston Educational Research Company.

When Pleasant Rowland retired from her position as head of American Girls, she turned her energies to philanthropy, using the fortune she had made to better her community. Along with her husband, Jerry Frautschi, the couple is active in civic affairs in their home city of

Madison, Wisconsin, and built Overture Hall there as a home for the symphony. They even had an organ built especially for the new concert hall. Why the arts?

When Pleasant Rowland was a little girl growing up in Chicago, her mother took her to children's concerts in the symphony hall there. "When I was a little girl, I just have this memory that will stay with me forever," she said in an interview with Madison Magazine. "I was probably eight or nine years old, and the symphony hall, as I recall then, was pale blue, and behind the orchestra was this gorgeous organ above the great symphony players. To me it was just this cathedral of a space. I remember because I was alone with my mother and not my sisters; it was a sort of grown-up special day."

Because her mother instilled a deep sense of excellence and moral and social values in her, Pleasant has made it her life's work to share her bounty through her American Girls Collection.

> FIRST THING IN THE MORNING, SHE DRESSES FOR WORK, ROLLS UP HER SLEEVES, EAGER TO GET STARTED. SHE SENSES THE WORTH OF HER WORK, IS IN NO HURRY TO CALL IT QUITS FOR THE DAY.
>
> PROVERBS 31:17-18 MSG

A Mother of Influence strives for excellence in all she does.

SACAGAWEA

1789 - 1814 or 1889

JEAN BAPTISTE AND LIZETTE CHARBONNEAU, ADOPTED SON, BAZIL, AND POSSIBLY FIVE OTHER CHIL-DREN. Sacagawea helped Lewis and Clark open up the American West for settlement and acted as a courageous role model for her own children.

Much like Joseph in the book of Genesis, Sacagawea was torn from her Shoshone family and taken captive by another tribe—Hidatsa warriors—who attacked at Three Forks, at the Missouri River headwaters in today's Montana. She survived, along with another captive girl. No one knows how long she lived with her enemies, but at some point, she and the other Shoshone girl were sold (or won by gambling) to Toussaint Charbonneau, a French-Canadian fur trapper and interpreter. He later married both of them.

At about the age of sixteen in 1805, Sacagawea and Charbonneau met with Meriwether Lewis and William Clark in North Dakota, where the famous explorers of the Northwest Passage were wintering at a fort near the Mandan tribe. In the spring, only two months after giving birth, Sacagawea, Charbonneau, and her infant son Baptiste, who had been born in February, set out with the explorers.

Legend says that Sacagawea was a guide for Lewis and Clark, but in reality, she was the only one who spoke the Shoshone language and would serve as their interpreter to acquire horses from her former people. She had only been about ten years old when she was first captured, so she could not have guided the expedition through the wilderness. The only reason Lewis and Clark allowed Charbonneau to accompany them was because of Sacagawea. In addition to acting as an interpreter, she could also identify and find edible roots, berries, and other vegetation that enhanced the men's diet. She even helped them catch small animals.

For the next two years, carrying Baptiste on her back in a papoose cradle, Sacagawea braved the same hardships as the men she accompanied to find a passable water route to the Pacific Ocean. Her very presence ensured the expedition's safety. When Lewis and Clark needed horses or other supplies, it was Sacagawea who would approach the various Indian tribes to bargain with them, using sign language when she could not understand their spoken words. These tribes assumed the white men meant no harm if an Indian woman and her child were traveling with the expedition.

Once as she rode in a pirogue—canoe with a sail—piloted by her husband near the Yellowstone River, high winds hit. The boat nearly overturned and was swamped with water.

THEN JOSEPH SAID TO HIS BROTHERS, "COME CLOSE TO ME." WHEN THEY HAD DONE SO, HE SAID, "I AM YOUR BROTHER JOSEPH, THE ONE YOU SOLD INTO EGYPT! AND NOW, DO NOT BE DISTRESSED AND DO NOT BE ANGRY WITH YOURSELVES FOR SELLING ME HERE, BECAUSE IT WAS TO SAVE LIVES THAT GOD SENT ME AHEAD OF YOU.

GENESIS 45:4-5 NIV

Captain Clark wrote in his journal about the incident, "The articles which floated out were nearly all caught by the squaw who was in the rear. This accident might have cost us dearly; for in this pirogue were embarked our papers, instruments, books, medicine, a great proportion of our merchandise."

"The Indian woman," Lewis wrote, "to whom I ascribe equal fortitude and resolution with any person on board at the time of the accident, caught and preserved most of the light articles which were washed over-board." Lewis and Clark were so grateful for her efforts that they named a river after her.

When the expedition finally reached Shoshone territory, Lewis and Clark, along with the young Native American woman, approached the tribe to barter for food. As they were speaking, Sacagawea realized that Chief Cameahwait or Black Bow, was her brother. They had not seen one another for at least four years. Overjoyed, they shared their stories, and Sacagawea learned that the rest of her family, except for Chief Cameahwait and an orphaned nephew named Bazil, had been killed.

Only the two of them had survived a vicious raid.

Seeing that she was overcome with emotion after learning of her family's fate, Lewis and Clark postponed their meeting with the Shoshone so that Sacagawea could mourn her loss. Soon, however, they found out that the Shoshone were in as dire need of food as the white men. It was reported that when one of the men shot a small animal, the warriors were so hungry that they ate the meat raw with their bare hands.

Sacagawea's brother promised to help supply the Anglo expedition but decided instead to send his men off to hunt buffalo. His sister found out he had broken his word and told her husband, Charbonneau. She wanted him to tell Lewis and Clark, but Sacagawea's husband hated any woman telling him what to do. Only nonchalantly did he pass on the information to Captain Lewis, who immediately called for a meeting with Chief Cameahwait. Around this time, both Lewis and Clark recorded in their journals that they observed Charbonneau striking Sacagawea several times, and he was soundly reprimanded by the explorers.

Sacagawea had cast her fate with the white men, but her intervention caused her brother to keep his word and call his people back to help the whites. It was a difficult decision for the Shoshone chief. It could spell doom for the starved tribe, but without their help, the expedition could also perish.

At long last, Sacagawea reached the Pacific Ocean with the Lewis and Clark expedition. She was frightened at the immensity of the vast body of water that stretched before her. Soon though, along with the men, she was wading through the salty waves, and she marveled when they found a stranded whale on the beach, which the men harvested for its supply of oil.

Sacagawea's story becomes a little hazy from this point. Some accounts say she died of a fever at the age of twenty-five. But the oral tradition of her tribe says that she returned to her people and lived on the Wind River Reservation until her death past the age of 100.

Like Joseph, ripped from his family and sent into captivity, Sacagawea not only survived, she flourished and gained the respect of the renowned explorers Lewis and Clark, just as Joseph became an invaluable member of Pharaoh's court. And like Joseph, she was recognized in her time, as well as in the years to come, for her courage, wisdom, and heroic character.

Sacagawea has been honored with more memorials than any other American woman in history. A river, two lakes, a mountain peak, and a mountain pass in Montana are named after her, and statues of Sacagawea with her son Baptiste on her back stand in a park in Bismarck, North Dakota, and Portland, Oregon, and a bronze statue was exhibited in 1904 at the World's Fair in St. Louis. There is also a bronze tablet, telling of Sacagawea at Three Forks, Montana; a monument for her was erected at Armstead, Montana; a water fountain marks her life at Lewiston, Idaho; and there's a cement shaft marking a grave assumed to be hers on the Shoshone reservation. In 2001 the U.S. government issued a golden dollar coin with her image and that of her infant son.

Although Captain Lewis only mentioned her once in his journals, Captain Clark seemed to hold the young Sacagawea, whom he nicknamed "Janey," in high esteem. Another expedition member by the name of Brackenridge wrote of her that she was "a good creature, of mild and gentle disposition, greatly attached to the whites, whose manners and dress she tries to imitate." Other historians have described her as modest, unselfish, and patient.

Without Sacagawea's help and sacrifice, it's doubtful that Lewis and Clark would have completed their journey across the Northwest Territory. Despite her life of adversity, including an abusive husband, this young mother rose above her circumstances and made a vital contribution to the exploration of the West, her own children, and her native people.

A Mother of Influence teaches her children how to survive adversity.

BARBARA BUSH

1925 -

PRESIDENT GEORGE W. BUSH AND GOVERNOR JEB
BUSH. By pouring her devotion
into her children, listening to them, and teaching them
to care about others, Barbara Bush raised two sons
who have served the public in political office.

᳁᳁

T he former First Lady Barbara Bush is the only woman other than
Abigail Adams who has been married to one president and given
birth to another. Another son is governor of Florida. Yet she
would rather be remembered as someone who loved her children and
cared for the needs of others.

Because her husband, George, was so busy building an oil company
and running for political office, Barbara Bush shouldered most of the
responsibility for raising their family. She was tough, but fair, and spent
as much time with her kids as possible.

In 1945, Barbara married George Bush, the first boy she'd ever
kissed, and dropped out of Smith College her sophomore year to devote
herself to her husband and children. Her son George W. Bush was born
while her husband completed his courses at Yale University, where he
graduated in 1948. Even then, her goal was to be the best parent possible.
After graduation, the couple moved with their infant son to Texas where
they had five more children: John (Jeb), Neil, Marvin, Dorothy, and
Robin.

As First Lady, Mrs. Bush's campaign for literacy was legendary, but
she believed it takes more than learning to read to be a better parent. She

felt parents needed to learn how to parent.

She told the *Chicago Tribune* in an interview, "There's not an awful lot we can do about that except try to train parents. Missouri, for instance, has a parenting program where they talk to mothers literally in clinics before they have the babies and teach them how to parent. I think our school systems have been at fault some. I think we have been at fault enormously. We expect our teachers to be mother and father and church and teach our children morals. I think a lot of our problems are because people don't listen to our children. It's not always easy. They're not always so brilliant that you want to spend hours with them."

MANY WOMEN DO NOBLE THINGS, BUT YOU SURPASS THEM ALL.

PROVERBS 31:29 NIV

Even when it wasn't easy, Barbara Bush put in the time with her children. Son Neil Bush suffered from dyslexia. The Chicago Tribune noted, "She expended more time and effort to help him overcome severe reading difficulty than many mothers spend on parenting, period."

In a 1989 letter to *Their World*, published by the National Center for Learning Disabilities, Mrs. Bush wrote, "George Bush and I know the frustration of living with an undiagnosed or untreated learning problem, and we know the great joy and relief that comes when help is finally found. I foresee the day when no American—neither child nor adult—will ever need to be limited in learning."

In addition to Neil's dyslexia, the Bush's youngest daughter, Robin, died of leukemia at the age of four. It is still difficult for them to talk about that time without tearing up. Because Barbara Bush has known heartache, she has a heart for others who suffer similar problems.

As First Lady, she was not interested in the latest fashions or choosing new china patterns. Instead, she was every American's white-haired grandmother—a size 14 who made no excuses for her wrinkles. Candid and forthright, her husband still calls her Miss Frank.

In her book *Simply Barbara Bush*, author Donnie Radcliffe wrote, "Here was a First Lady who professed to care more about where people slept at night and what they ate, whether their children learned to read and if anybody was looking after them, than whether she gained thirteen pounds, wore the same old clothes, or looked a fright in pictures." Barbara Bush has been called one of the most popular First Ladies in history.

When George W. and Jeb Bush followed their father into politics, their mother became one of their biggest supporters. Her positive, upbeat, can-do attitude rubbed off on her sons, and when they faced major tragedies in office, it was their mother's backbone of steel that influenced them. George W. Bush exhibited his mother's strength in the aftermath of 9/11 and the war on terror, and Jeb Bush never wavered while dealing with the enormous loss of life and property damage when Florida was hit by four major hurricanes in one season.

Because Barbara Bush chose motherhood over a career, she gave the world two sons who have served America with honor.

**A Mother of Influence teaches
her children to serve others.**

MARGARETHA SCHMIDT HEINZ

Unknown

HENRY JOHN HEINZ. A strong woman of faith, Margaretha

Heinz was credited by her entrepreneurial son with

his success in life.

The basement reeked of horseradish—hot and pungent—as a young Henry J. Heinz ground the spices to help make his mother's pickles, which were the rave of Pittsburgh, Pennsylvania. When his German mother, Margaretha, finished canning her pickles, eight-year-old Henry hustled through the streets of the city, delivering them to the buyers, as well as selling any excess produce the family had grown.

Like many successful entrepreneurs and industrious businessmen before and after him, Henry J. Heinz was the firstborn of eight children and arrived on October 11, 1844, in a city teeming with entrepreneurial spirit. As unlikely as it seems, horseradish would become Henry's ticket to fame as a canned food manufacturer, and his fortune would rise and fall with the hot spice.

First, the young man needed business training. He attended Duff's Business College, finishing his coursework before hiring on as a bookkeeper at his father's brickyard. When he was old enough, he was made a partner, and even though he went back to his real career, which started in his mother's basement, it was said he remained interested in the brick business and became somewhat of an expert. He even chose the bricks used in the building of his company.

But the hot spice of his mother's popular horseradish was in his blood; it and other vegetables became his passion. With Yankee ingenuity, Henry J. Heinz developed a system of hotbeds and intensive gardening methods to grow two and even three vegetable crops per year. By 1860, several women were in his employ, and he was delivering three wagonloads of produce per week to grocers in the Pittsburgh area.

At the age of twenty-five, Henry hooked up with a friend and business partner—Clarence Noble—to grow and sell grated horseradish. One of the first in the food industry to market purity in his products, Heinz brilliantly decided to switch to clear glass bottles to prove to customers how fresh and superior his horseradish was.

Soon the partners had outgrown their home gardens and built a food-packing factory on the Allegheny River in Pennsylvania to can horseradish and other products in their clear bottles. Because Henry J. Heinz was such a great salesman, the company gained a solid reputation. There was only one problem: an overabundance of horseradish. By 1875, the price of the hot spice plunged to almost nothing and nobody wanted to pay his prices when they could practically get it free.

By the age of thirty-one, Henry J. Heinz and his partners were in deep financial trouble. In November of 1875 he wrote that he was deeply in debt and had "not a penny to meet it with." Not long after that, Heinz's company went belly up. A newspaper article at the time called them a "Trio in a Pickle."

Their problem was cash flow. Because there was a bumper crop of cucumbers in 1875, Heinz had mistakenly decided to expand, without guaranteeing enough financing to increase the factory's capacity. Although Heinz later paid his share of the company's debts in full, he was personally liable for about $20,000.

However, Henry J. Heinz's mother had not raised a quitter. The next year, he reopened his bottled food business with his brother John and cousin Frederick as partners. Unlike the deplorable conditions of many factories of the day, Heinz motivated his employees by treating them well and maintaining good, clean working conditions. It worked. Because of Heinz's concern with the welfare of his employees, no doubt inspired by his godly mother, he never suffered any labor troubles.

In his latest business venture, Heinz kept a close watch on his money and added a ketchup product line so that they would not be dependent on just one crop. He always insisted on the finest, purest ingredients for his food products, and the business expanded with celery sauce, pickled cucumbers, sauerkraut, vinegar, jams, jellies, and other condiments.

SINCE MY MOTHER BORE ME YOU HAVE BEEN MY GOD.

PSALM 22:10 NRSV

One of Heinz's greatest innovations was the "factory tour" so that ordinary people could witness the packing process, and he could showcase his clean factory and fresh ingredients. The public relations feat was so successful that other manufacturing companies soon followed in his footsteps.

The Heinz Company became so successful that at one point, it provided more than half the ketchup around the globe. In 1886, Heinz said after making the first overseas sale, "Our field is the world." He then created an international sales force that sold Heinz products on every continent.

Heinz had already proved he was a marketing genius with the factory tour, but he felt that any great company also needed a slogan, something that would be instantly recognizable to the consumer.

"While most advertising slogans come from 'creatives' on Madison Avenue," said a spokesman for the H.J. Heinz Company, "the creation of the renowned Heinz advertising phrase is surrounded in great mystery. A visionary, Heinz was inspired by the number 57. In reality, when Henry Heinz created '57 Varieties' in 1896, the company already had more than 60 varieties of products. For reasons no one will ever know, Henry Heinz' mind was stuck on the number 57, and his phrase has stuck ever since."

Even though the company produced more than 57 products, it didn't seem to matter, and the slogan stuck. Heinz 57 is still used in its advertising campaigns today.

Although his business was a large part of his life, Heinz never forgot his mother's faith. Because of her influence, he served as a Sunday school superintendent for twenty-five years and took an active role in state, national, and international Sunday school organizations. He had planned to attend a Sunday school convention in New York on the day he died of pneumonia on May 14, 1919, at his home in Pittsburgh.

Perhaps more than any other document, the will of Henry J. Heinz revealed his deep faith and his feelings for his mother. In it he wrote, "Looking forward to the time when my earthly career will end, I desire to set forth at the very beginning of this will, as the most important item in it, a confession of my faith in Jesus Christ as my Savior. I also bear witness to the fact that throughout my life, in which there were unusual joys and sorrows, I have been wonderfully sustained by my faith in God through Jesus Christ. This legacy was left to me by my consecrated mother, a woman of strong faith, and to it I attribute any success I have attained."

A Mother of Influence leaves her children a legacy of faith.

DOROTHY MAY
SKAGGS

1928 - 2001

RICKY SKAGGS. Dorothy May Skaggs' gospel roots

inspired and were a major musical influence on her son Ricky's

successful bluegrass career.

⟨∞⟩

B y the time Ricky Skaggs was three years old, he was already a pro, singing gospel and country music with his parents, Hobart and Dorothy May Skaggs, at social gatherings near their home in Lawrence County, Kentucky. And by the age of five when most kids are learning to read, he was already singing and playing the mandolin onstage!

"Me and my mom would do a lot of duets," Ricky told *The Big Book of Bluegrass*, "and my dad would sing baritone or bass, so we would have lead and tenor and bass, and it would sound real haunting and neat. We used to work a lot of churches, and we played in high schools and at pie suppers and theaters and stuff." It was a fun time for all of them.

Recognizing Ricky's exceptional talent, the family decided to move to Nashville when he was only seven, with the goal of getting him on the Grand Ole Opry. That door wouldn't budge (Ricky finally became an Opry member in 1982 at the age of twenty-seven), but Mom and Dad were able to set him up for a guest appearance on the Flatt & Scruggs syndicated TV show. Two years later, the family moved back to Kentucky and continued to encourage Ricky's talents.

As he grew older, Ricky's heroes in the music business were the Stanley Brothers — Ralph and Carter — who were prominent bluegrass musicians. When he was a young teenager, Ricky practiced and practiced until he could sing and pick bluegrass just like his heroes. During those years he also mastered the fiddle and guitar, in addition to his mandolin.

While performing with his parents when he was in high school, Ricky met another kid who also wanted to be a bluegrass musician — Keith Whitley. With Keith's brother on banjo, Ricky, Keith, and Keith's brother formed a trio, and soon they were playing on local radio shows.

Learning that their hero Ralph Stanley was giving a concert in West Virginia, fifteen-year-old Ricky and his friend Keith decided to drive there to hear him play. Stanley was late, so the club's owner asked Ricky and Keith to fill in until Stanley made it.

"We got up and entertained the crowd, and they were liking it — and in walks Ralph Stanley, my hero," Ricky said. "He set his banjo case down . . . and I glanced over at him out of the corner of my eye. He wasn't really smiling, he was looking off somewhere like he was reminiscing. Afterward he said, 'Boys, the first time I saw y'all it just brought back so many memories of me and Carter.'"

Their performance earned an invitation to join Stanley's band, the Clinch Mountain Boys. But because Ricky was only fifteen and still in high school, he could only work with the band during holidays and summers. In that two years from 1970 to 1972 Ricky found out what he was capable of.

"It was a good training ground," Ricky said, "and I learned a lot of things about feel and music — I learned what not to play. Those were really great days."

Unable to make a living as a bluegrass musician, Ricky took a job repairing boilers for a power company in Washington, D.C. He hated it with a passion! So in 1973, he leaped at the chance to play fiddle and sing again as a member of the bluegrass band Country Gentlemen. By the age of twenty, when Ricky quit the Country Gentlemen, he was well-known and had a solid reputation. Lots of groups wanted him to work with them. He cut a solo album for Rebel Records before joining J. D. Crowe and the New South, a progressive bluegrass band.

Ricky finally formed his own group, Boone Creek, after playing with New South for a year. Vince Gill played bass with them for a while, and they cut two albums before the group broke up in 1978.

Next stop on his career path was working with Emmylou Harris, whom Ricky had gotten to know as a friend when he was playing with Country Gentlemen and she was performing in Washington, D.C. He joined her band and advised her while she made her first album. Ricky performed on many of Emmylou's early albums, including the Grammy Award-winning *Roses in the Snow*.

Ricky Skaggs finally launched his solo career in 1980, when his album called *Sweet Temptation* was hailed by music critics, and in 1982 he landed a contract with Epic Records.

Some have said that Ricky Skaggs has done more for country and bluegrass music than any other performer and was instrumental in turning Nashville from country-pop back to its mountain roots—the music his mama had taught him to sing when he was just a toddler.

The LORD will command His lov- ingkindness in the day- time; and His song will be with me in the night, a prayer to the God of my life.

Psalm 42:8 nasb

"Without the pioneering work of Ricky Skaggs, there probably wouldn't be any new country or new traditionalist music," Andrew Vaughan wrote in *Who's Who in New Country*. "Before George Strait was popular, before Reba McEntire was a superstar, before The Judds cap- tured hearts with their mountain harmonies, Skaggs was breaking through country music's lowest ebb. The late seventies and early eighties had seen country go pop. . . . But Skaggs re-introduced the backwoods sound, and with an impeccably tight band and clear, snappy bluegrass- influenced productions, his records and live shows came like a breath of fresh air through a stagnant Nashville smog."

As a result Ricky Skaggs has won practically every award, and his songs and albums have topped the music charts. He's won eight Country Music Association Awards, four Grammy Awards, and *Billboard Magazine's* Artist of the Year.

In 2002, Ricky donated the proceeds from his recording of "Weapon of Prayer" to the Presidential Prayer Team. The bluegrass song was recorded by Ricky and Kentucky Thunder after the tragic events of September 11. The song, written by Ira and Charlie Louvin and pub- lished by Acuff-Rose Music, Inc., was produced along with a multimedia event to honor the victims and families of those affected by the terrorist attacks. Ricky is also a member of the Honorary Committee of The Presidential Prayer Team, whose members pray daily for the president and other American leaders, as well as special issues like national elec- tions.

Ricky Skaggs' love of bluegrass music and his talent for writing and singing were inherited from his beloved mother, Dorothy, who was also a talented performer and writer. Her song "All I Ever Loved Was You," has been recorded by numerous bluegrass groups, including Ralph Stanley and the Clinch Mountain Boys, Keith Whitley and Ricky Skaggs on the album *Second Generation Bluegrass*, and Shenandoah on *Keith Whitley: A Tribute Album*.

On February 8, 2004, Ricky Skaggs added one more award to his collection: the Grammy Award for best country performance by a duo or group with vocal, for "A Simple Life," with Kentucky Thunder. His mama would have been proud.

A Mother of Influence sings songs of faith to her children.

ANNA ANDERSON

Unknown

MARIAN ANDERSON. Because of the sacrifices Anna Anderson

made for her daughter, she would live to see Marian acclaimed

as one of the world's greatest voices of all time.

World-renowned contralto Marian Anderson was once interviewed by a reporter and asked to name the greatest moment of her life. She had many to choose from. The reporter expected her to name the private concert she gave at the White House for the President and Mrs. Roosevelt and the King and Queen of England, or perhaps the night she received the $10,000 Bok Award as the person who had done the most for her hometown of Philadelphia, or when she sang before a crowd of 75,000 on Easter morning at the Lincoln Memorial.

Instead, Marian Anderson surprised the reporter with her quick answer. "The greatest moment in my life," she said, "was the day I went home and told my mother she wouldn't have to take in washing anymore."

Born on February 17, 1902, in a Philadelphia ghetto, Marian Anderson—the oldest of three girls—was destined to become one of the first classical music singers to break the color barrier. Her mother, Anna D. Anderson, had taught school in Lynchburg, Virginia, before she married John Berkeley Anderson, but when she moved to Philadelphia with him, there were no teaching jobs available. Instead, to help feed her family, Anna took in laundry, did housework for people, and later when her daughters were older, she took a job as a cleaning woman at Wanamaker's Department Store. Marian's father worked for a company that sold ice and coal in the local area.

The family lived in South Philly near her father's parents, and Marian held warm memories of her early childhood. Her father, a member and officer of the large Union Baptist Church, took Marian to his church when she was just a toddler—her musical ability was encouraged and flourished there. At the age of six, Marian began singing in the junior choir, belting out Negro spirituals and hymns. That early choral experience at church helped develop her amazing vocal range, which spanned three octaves—from low D to high C—at its peak.

When Marian was ten, her father was injured on the job and could never work again. The Anderson family moved into her paternal grandparents' home, where John died of a brain tumor when Marian was only twelve. The burden of caring for her family fell on her mother's shoulders. Five years later, when Marian was only seventeen, Anna came down with a serious case of the flu. Now it was Marian's turn to support the family.

When she was about fifteen, Marian wanted so badly to take voice lessons that she tried to enroll in a local music school, only to be turned away. "We don't take colored," she was told. It was the first time she had ever been a victim of such blatant racism.

It "was a tremendously great shock," she said in an interview. "So you learn. I don't say you ever accept, but you learn that there are people who are like that."

At William Penn High School, trying to be practical, Marian enrolled in secretarial classes—typing and shorthand—so when she graduated she'd be able to help support her mother and sisters. And sometimes she was paid a small fee for singing at churches or neighborhood activities, and she shared everything she made with her family.

Since she wasn't allowed to take instruction at the local music school, a family friend introduced her to soprano Mary Saunders Patterson, a locally famous soprano who waived her normal fee for voice lessons.

When Marian sang for some visiting dignitaries at her high school, one of them, a Dr. Rohrer, urged her principal to allow Marian to transfer to a college prep school—South Philadelphia High School for Girls— from which she graduated on June 20, 1921. During that time, she also sang with the Philadelphia Choral Society.

By the age of eighteen, Marian had outgrown her local voice teachers. With her mother ill again and her father dead, she was doing all she could to support her family and couldn't afford a more expensive coach. But her church members came to the rescue by raising the money for vocal lessons with Giuseppe Boghetti, an Italian-born vocal coach who had trained some of the leading concert performers of that time.

After high school graduation, Marian decided to tackle her first recital before a predominantly white audience in Manhattan's Town Hall. Attendance was low, and she was humiliated by the critical reviews that ripped apart her mechanical pronunciation of foreign words. For more than a year, she did not sing in public and almost abandoned her dream of becoming a concert performer.

> [JESUS SAID,] "GIVE, AND IT WILL BE GIVEN TO YOU. . . . FOR BY YOUR STANDARD OF MEASURE IT WILL BE MEASURED TO YOU IN RETURN."
>
> LUKE 6:38 NASB

It was Marian's mother who made her pick up her tattered pride to try again. Anna was ill, yet she went to work anyway because the family needed her paycheck. Marian vowed she would become a success so that her mother would never have to work again. Taking note of her critics' comments, Marian began to train again with Boghetti and took Italian, German, and French lessons as well.

Her efforts paid off. In 1925, following a recital at New York's Town Hall, Boghetti entered Marian in a national music contest, and she walked away with first prize—a chance to sing with the New York Philharmonic Orchestra.

Because of Anna Anderson's sacrifice and faith in her daughter's talent, Marian continued her musical training and in 1929 went to Europe to study. After a concert in Salzburg, Austria, where the famed conductor Arturo Toscanini heard Marian sing, he told her that she had "a voice heard but once in a century."

She became a star in Europe, but in America, she was not allowed to perform at many venues because of the separation of the races. In 1939, the nation was outraged when the Daughters of the American Revolution (DAR) refused to allow Marian to sing at Constitution Hall. Because of their prejudice, First Lady Eleanor Roosevelt resigned from the organization.

At the request of President and Mrs. Roosevelt, the Secretary of the Interior offered the use of the Lincoln Memorial for a free public recital on Easter Sunday. At first, Marian Anderson was averse to the invitation, fearing she would become a flashpoint for racial prejudice. The "tall, tobacco-colored girl with large, melting eyes" had never retaliated against racism with anger, but rather with grace and distinction, attributing prejudice to ignorance. Finally, she agreed to sing and stand as a symbol of democracy.

The air seemed electrically charged as more than seventy-five thousand people braved the chill April morning in 1939 to hear the rich voice of Marian Anderson. Behind her sat the massive statue of President Abraham Lincoln, who had signed the Emancipation Proclamation, freeing her ancestors. From her viewpoint at the top of that long flight of stairs, the crowd seemed massive.

"It was a tremendous thing and my heart beat like mad—it's never beat like that before—loud and strong and as though it wanted to say something," Anderson said in an interview. "I don't like to use the word protesting but my reaction was, what have I done that should bring this onto my heart? I was not trying to cut anybody down. I just wanted to sing and to share."

Allen Hughes wrote in *Musical America* that the people had come "because they sensed somehow that Marian Anderson stood for something good. She represented something beyond the range of mere professional achievement, some undefinable thing that had to do with them, something that was, perhaps, eternal."

After her concert at the Lincoln Memorial, Marian Anderson not only became a symbol for the struggles of Black-American artists, she also became a superstar. Now she could command the kind of fees that would allow her to take care of her mother and the rest of her family. Her mother could retire.

During her more than forty-year career, Marian Anderson broke the color barrier and won the world's acclaim by performing for several U.S. Presidents, as well as numerous members of European royalty. She also served a one-year term as a delegate to the United Nations—all because of her mother's sacrifices, her tough encouragement after career setbacks, and her steadfast faith that Marian would succeed.

A Mother of Influence makes
sacrifices for her children.

IDA STOVER EISENHOWER

1862 - 1946

DWIGHT D. EISENHOWER. As a Mennonite pacifist,

Ida Eisenhower taught her son, who would lead troops in battle

and become President of the United States, to control his anger

and seek the way of peace.

❧

As Dwight D. Eisenhower waited to take the oath of office to become the thirty-fourth president of the United States, the words of his parents echoed in his mind: "Opportunity is all around. Reach out and take it." This former World War II general would serve two terms as president, fight the spread of Communism, and lead his country through the end of the Korean War. How ironic then that his mother had been a Mennonite pacifist!

Ida Stover had witnessed the destruction that the Civil War brought upon her town and family. Because her parents died when she was quite young, she and her seven brothers went to live with her grandparents who raised them as Mennonites. In their home she learned to study and memorize the Bible and was taught the value of pacifism. Later she went to a Mennonite college where she fell in love with and married David Eisenhower. A few years later, Ida gave birth to a son, Dwight, or Ike as many called him.

While Ike's father could be angry and harsh, his mother lavished joy and optimism on her family. One of the most defining moments of his life, Eisenhower once said, was when his father whipped him severely for throwing a temper tantrum. His tender-hearted mother came along soon afterward and lovingly tended to his wounds. She also gently shared Scripture about

> **THOSE WHO CON-TROL THEIR ANGER HAVE GREAT UNDER-STANDING; THOSE WITH A HASTY TEMPER WILL MAKE MISTAKES.**
>
> PROVERBS 14:29 NLT

restraining his anger in the future.

Both David and Ida Eisenhower strongly believed in allowing Ike and his siblings to choose their own way in life, but their beliefs were thoroughly tested when Ike decided to enter military school. As a pacifist Ida was against the use of military power, but still she allowed her son to make his own career choice.

When General Eisenhower was Supreme Commander of the Allied invasion of Europe during World War II, he was faced with the responsibility of making one of the most far-reaching decisions ever posed to a single man: the decision to change the date of D-Day at the last moment. The consequences of a wrong decision were so overwhelming, in his opinion, that he felt crushed by the weight of responsibility. Still, he was the Supreme Commander and the only man who could make the decision that would impact millions of lives.

"I knew I did not have the required wisdom," he later wrote. "But turned to God. I asked God to give me the wisdom. I yielded myself to Him. I surrendered myself. And He gave me clear guidance. He gave me insight to see what was right, and He endowed me with courage to make my decision. And finally He gave me peace of mind in the knowledge that, having been guided by God to the decision, I could leave the results to Him." History confirms that his choice was correct.

Although General Eisenhower spent most of his career in the military, when he became president, his decisions were usually guided by the way of peace. It was Ike who achieved the truce that ended the Korean War, and he was always working to reduce tensions between the U.S. and Russia during the Cold War. Although Eisenhower believed in maintaining adequate military strength, he did not consider the use of military power to be the first option. He once said, "Though force can protect in emergency, only justice, fairness, consideration and cooperation can finally lead men to the dawn of eternal peace."

When his mother Ida died, Eisenhower singled her out as a woman known for her serenity and tolerance. Through living the truth of what she believed and giving her son the freedom to choose, Ida brought peace to the world.

A Mother of Influence teaches her children to control their tempers.

CATHERINE JANE CARMICHAEL

Unknown -1913

AMY CARMICHAEL. Catherine Carmichael taught her daughter

Amy to love and trust God for all her needs.

⸎

Sitting in the middle of the bare floor, surrounded by a large group of chattering Indian children, a white mother rocked her most recently rescued child. So many children had been snatched from a life of temple prostitution that Amy Carmichael, missionary to India, had stopped counting. As a single woman, Amy never dreamed that her mother's training would prove to be so very important to her.

Amy's mother, Catherine Jane Carmichael, felt she was called by God to the gift of motherhood. She operated under one rule: to train up her children so that each would know, love, and serve God. It was a hands-on experience for her children.

During Amy's childhood, the loving, nurturing Catherine constantly read stories, sang songs, and played with her seven children. When Amy recalled her early days, she remembered how her mother always helped her children get "endless fun out of life."

The other side of Catherine's training consisted of a deep personal relationship with God, dependency on God through faith and prayer, and helping the poor and needy. When the family had a need for something, she would pray with Amy and her siblings and then rejoice with them as God provided. Often, she would send them out with soup in hand for the sick in their neighborhood. By involving her children in charitable acts, they learned firsthand about faith and Christlike servanthood.

[JESUS SAID,] "GO YE THEREFORE, AND TEACH ALL NATIONS, BAPTIZING THEM IN THE NAME OF THE FATHER, AND OF THE SON, AND OF THE HOLY GHOST: TEACHING THEM TO OBSERVE ALL THINGS WHATSOEVER I HAVE COMMANDED YOU: AND, LO, I AM WITH YOU ALWAYS, EVEN UNTO THE END OF THE WORLD."

MATTHEW 28:19- 20 KJV

Letting her children venture into the world was not so easy for Catherine, but she did it with amazing outcomes. When Amy was a teenager, the young girl wanted to minister in the slums of Belfast near their home. Catherine, to the shock of the other mothers, allowed Amy to go. As a result, many of the young women Amy met were hungry for a relationship with Christ and accompanied Amy to church.

When Amy felt called as a missionary to India, Catherine faced the biggest test of her motherhood. Amy asked her mother's permission. Catherine not only gave it but also bestowed a prayer of blessing on her saying, "Yes my dearest, Amy. [God] has lent you to me all these years . . . my heart unfailingly says, Go ye."

Amy Carmichael sailed to India, remembering all her mother had taught her. She remembered her mother's training as she prayed for her own limited finances on the mission field. She remembered as she cared for each child that lived with her. She remembered as she battled a disease called neuralgia that attacked her nerves, causing so much pain and weakness that she would be bedridden for weeks. Even when other Christians said she was crazy for staying in India, Amy remembered her mother's convictions and remained firm in the Lord and true to her calling as a missionary. Under the influence of her mother's faith, Amy made the world a kinder place.

A Mother of Influence nurtures her children and releases them to God's care.

HELENA

250 - 330 A.D.

CONSTANTINE THE GREAT. When Helena chose

to forgive those who had wronged her, she taught

her son Constantine the better way of love.

⌒✖︎⌒

It's a very old story. A Roman soldier, Constantius Chlorus, falls in love with and marries a young woman named Helena, a woman of low social standing and humble background. They have a son. Then the soldier is offered power—real power—to be appointed by Caesar to serve under the Emperor Diocletian.

But there's a catch. Constantius was ordered to divorce Helena and marry the daughter of a high-ranking military officer. He is torn, but his desire for power wins the struggle. After he leaves his wife, she is sent into exile, alone and abandoned. Her son is to live at the court of Galerius, held as a kind of insurance so that his father Constantius would do what he was told.

What were Helena's options? She could have chosen to hate her husband and become bitter, plotting revenge. She could have given up on life, believing the lie that her circumstances defined her as worthless. Helena chose to restore rather than avenge or destroy. Her choice influenced her son, Constantine, who in turn changed the history of the world.

After his father's death, Constantine, now a soldier, came into power. His first act was to bring his mother, Helena, whom he loved and respected, out of exile and into his home. Not long after that, both he and his mother became Christians.

Before Constantine came to power, Christians had experienced a time of great persecution. The Emperor Diocletian, who believed that the end

> **[Jesus said,] "In prayer there is a connection between what God does and what you do. You can't get forgiveness from God, for instance, without also forgiving others."**
>
> Matthew 6:14 MSG

always justified the means, was willing to do anything to bring all Roman soldiers and citizens under his control. He required everyone who came before his throne to lay prostrate and call him "Lord and Master."

There was, however, one group of people who would not conform—Christians. So Diocletian issued decrees calling for the torture and death of all Christians who would not turn away from Christ and worship him as Emperor. When Constantine came to power, he not only ended the persecution of Christians but also declared Christianity as the religion of the state.

Aided by his mother, Constantine set out to right the wrongs of those who had ruled before him and restore the people of Rome. Helena experienced one of the most memorable events of her life at this time. She made a journey to Palestine, and it is said that she desired to pray at the sites where Jesus walked. Upon her return to Rome, she advised her son Constantine in the building of Christian churches and the restoration of historical biblical sites.

As Helena encouraged and helped Constantine in his good works, she also went out and ministered to the poor and the needy herself. It is said by Eusebius, a writer at that time, that she helped not only individuals but entire communities of those who were destitute.

What would have been the fate of Western Civilization had Helena chosen a different response to the unfair events that had been thrust upon her? There are many historical accounts of promiscuous women in the history of Rome, attempting to ascend the ladder of success by moving from one leader to another. Many powerful Roman women even killed their own family members to get what they wanted. There are few who chose the path of forgiveness as Helena did.

As she chose restoration, she became restored herself, and influenced her son to choose Christ. When Helena died, she was beloved by many, having a Catholic feast day and Roman town named after her.

A Mother of Influence models forgiveness for her children.

MONICA

332 - 387 A.D.

SAINT AUGUSTINE. Monica's prayers for her son Augustine finally

caused him to surrender his life to Christ, becoming one of the church's

greatest defenders of right doctrine.

⟨∞⟩

Augustine had come to the end of his road. He had been running away for years—from responsibility, his family, and what he knew to be the truth. What stopped this man's racing sandals? His mother Monica's passion and burden to see each member of her family become Christians.

Monica was born to wealthy Christian parents in Tagasta, North Africa. A kind family servant also taught Monica to believe in Christ. But things took a harsh turn when Monica's parents arranged her marriage to Patricus, who later turned out to be a violent and immoral man. He was not a believer and led an adulterous life.

Monica decided to follow the call of ministry to her family by doing what Paul said in the Bible—live your life in a way that will draw your husband and in this case, family, to Christ. She displayed loving behavior and was noted for being a peacemaker. Her character was known by many to be one free of bitterness and gossip. She took every opportunity to show and teach her children about the love of Christ. When she didn't see results, she refused to give up and patiently continued to pray. Even as her precious son Augustine walked away from Christ, he could hear her weeping and praying for him—and it changed him.

Augustine never forgot his mother's prayers for him. He went his own way for many years but finally came to know Christ as his own personal

> **WIVES, IN THE SAME WAY BE SUBMISSIVE TO YOUR HUSBANDS SO THAT, IF ANY OF THEM DO NOT BELIEVE THE WORD, THEY MAY BE WON OVER WITHOUT WORDS BY THE BEHAVIOR OF THEIR WIVES, WHEN THEY SEE THE PURITY AND REVERENCE OF YOUR LIVES.**
>
> 1 PETER 3:1- 2 NIV

Savior. He wrote about his mother's influence in one of his famous works called "Confessions." He said that his mother's grief and prayers for him were what helped bring him back to Christ.

After his conversion, Augustine grew in faith and became one of the most influential Christians of all times. He became Bishop of Hippo in 395 A.D. and remained so until his death. A brilliant theologian, he constantly battled false doctrine. In fact, his writings have shaped the ideas and doctrines of the western church today.

Monica's persistence in faith paid off. Augustine was not the only one who became a Christian. Monica's Christlike life and patient prayers brought her mother-in-law to Jesus as well. Finally, near the end of his life, her husband, Patricus, also gave his heart to Christ.

A Mother of Influence prays for the salvation of her children.

FLORA AUGUSTA HAMILTON LEWIS

Unknown

C. S. LEWIS. Flora's cheerful and tranquil personality left a lasting impression on her son "Jack," as Clive Staples Lewis was called, although she died of cancer when he was only nine.

❦

One dreary night in Belfast, Northern Ireland, Jack cried in his bed because of a dreadful headache, as well as a toothache. He wanted the soothing presence of his mother, but she did not come. Flora also was ill. All night, lying in pain, the little nine-year-old boy heard doctors coming and going in the big house, whispered conversations, and the opening and shutting of doors.

"It seemed to last for hours," he said in his autobiography, *Surprised by Joy: The Shape of My Life*. "And then my father, in tears, came into my room and began to try to convey to my terrified mind things it had never conceived before. It was in fact cancer. . . . My father never fully recovered from this loss."

But in those short nine years of his life, Flora made a profound impression on her son, who would one day grow up to write the best-loved children's Christian fantasy series, *The Chronicles of Narnia*.

His mother, Flora, the daughter of a clergyman and an intelligent mathematician, and father, Albert, a solicitor, could not have been more different. Jack's mother had a sunny fun-loving personality; his father was emotionally temperamental and prone to explosive anger.

"My father's people were true Welshmen," he wrote, "sentimental, passionate, and rhetorical, easily moved both to anger and to tenderness;

men who laughed and cried a great deal and who had not much of the talent for happiness." In speaking of his mother's family, he wrote in *Surprised by Joy: The Shape of My Life*, "The Hamiltons were a cooler race. Their minds were critical and ironic and they had the talent for happiness in a high degree—went straight for it as experienced travelers go for the best seat in a train. From my earliest years I was aware of the vivid contrast between my mother's cheerful and tranquil affection and the ups and downs of my father's emotional life." Because he felt such calmness around his mother, throughout his lifetime C. S. Lewis distrusted highly charged emotions and considered himself a more reasonable and rational man.

When Flora was still alive, Jack's early childhood with his older brother, Warren, was a time spent reading, drawing imaginative pictures, and playing in the Irish countryside. As their father prospered, they moved into the "new house" when Jack was seven, with its "long corridors, empty sunlit rooms, upstairs indoor silences, attics explored in solitude, distant noises of gurgling cisterns and pipes, and the noise of wind under the tiles." He once wrote that the house itself became a major character in many of his books.

An author in the making, Jack claimed an attic room for his own in which to dream. It was there that he kept his pen, inkpot, writing books, and paintbox. Here he wrote and illustrated his first stories—stories of "chivalrous mice and rabbits who rode out" dressed in knights' armor to slay evil cats.

It was a time of warm safety, and then his mother died. "With my mother's death," he wrote in his autobiography, "all settled happiness, all that was tranquil and reliable, disappeared from my life. There was to be much fun, many pleasures, many stabs of joy; but no more of the old security. It was sea and islands now; the great continent had sunk like Atlantis."

As his mother had grown worse, his father had become more explosive, acting unpredictably and with anger toward his sons. "Thus by a peculiar cruelty of fate, during those months the unfortunate man, had he but known it, was really losing his sons as well as his wife," Jack wrote.

Quite soon after his mother's passing, Jack was sent off to boarding school at a time when he surely needed reassurance and love. He would attend numerous schools and colleges and entered Oxford in 1917, only to be called in 1918 to fight in World War I. He was wounded in France and spent months recuperating before returning to Oxford, where he spent the rest of his academic life.

Although his mother had grounded him in her faith when he was a child, as a young man of twenty-eight, he considered himself to be an atheist, which was the accepted norm for most young intellectuals of that era.

However, a conversation one day with colleague Thomas Dewar Weldon launched him on a spiritual search that lasted for three years. During a summer vacation, C. S. Lewis had a mystical experience that he could not explain, but it led him to accept God's existence.

Lewis wrote in his autobiography, "I gave in, and admitted that God was God, and knelt and prayed: perhaps, that night, the most dejected and reluctant convert in all England." Several months later, he wrote to a friend that he had passed from believing in God to believing in Christ. He had become a Christian. By the end of 1931, he joined the Anglican church, and prayer became a lifelong habit.

Due to the influence of his mother's faith and cheerful disposition early in his life, C. S. "Jack" Lewis found his true calling as a Christian apologist and famed author, whose books are still best-sellers, including such classics as *The Screwtape Letters*, *Mere Christianity*, and *The Chronicles of Narnia*.

[PAUL SAID,] "FOR WHAT IS OUR HOPE, OR JOY, OR CROWN OF REJOICING? ARE NOT EVEN YE IN THE PRESENCE OF OUR LORD JESUS CHRIST AT HIS COMING? FOR YE ARE OUR GLORY AND JOY."

1 THESSALONIANS 2:19,-20 KJV

A Mother of Influence shares joy with her children while she can.

FRANCES "FANNY" SMITH NIGHTINGALE

Unknown

FLORENCE NIGHTINGALE. Despite Fanny Nightingale's aversion to Florence's desire for the nursing profession, she did model charity to the poor for her daughter, and Florence became known as the founder of modern nursing, as well as a spiritual mother to the British army.

⬥⬥⬥

One night in 1837, at the age of sixteen, a tall girl with gray eyes and long chestnut hair heard the first of four callings from God to pursue a mission for Him.

"God spoke to me," Florence Nightingale wrote, "and called me to His service."

However, as daughters of a wealthy family, Florence and her elder sister, Parnethope, were expected to pursue the womanly subjects of music, art, history, and languages, as well as learning to entertain, sew and embroider, and marry well. Florence would rather have studied mathematics, but she was forbidden until her Aunt Mai persuaded Fanny to give her daughter the chance. Still, the lessons lasted only for a year.

Even though Florence had not yet been allowed to follow her dream of becoming a nurse, considered a scandalous profession for an educated woman of her class, her mother did impress on her the importance of showing charity to the poor. When Florence's mother visited the rural slums and served soup to the destitute and passed out small pieces of silver, Florence was allowed to accompany her. It made a lasting impression.

The young woman continued to beg her parents to support her nursing mission, but instead, they sent her on a series of world tours to places like Germany, Rome, and Egypt, thinking she would get over such nonsense. Instead, it only strengthened her desire to follow God into the medical mission field. Her diaries from that time reveal her struggle between trying to please her mother and father and pleasing God.

> [JESUS SAID,] "BLESSED ARE THE MERCIFUL: FOR THEY SHALL OBTAIN MERCY."
>
> MATTHEW 5:7 KJV

During her visit to Egypt, she met the Sisters of Saint Vincent de Paul and was greatly influenced by their sacrifices for others. Then in 1851, a friend sent her information about the Institution of Protestant Deaconesses at Kaiserwerth, near Düsseldorf in Prussia. She later entered that institution for three months of nursing training. Despite the filthy conditions and heavy workload there, a nervous condition, which had plagued her for years—probably because of her conflicted emotions—improved.

She briefly worked for the Sisters of Mercy in a hospital near Paris, before returning to London, where in 1853 she became the unpaid superintendent of a "women's hospital"—the Establishment for Gentlewomen during Illness.

But when she learned there was a severe shortage of medical help available to British soldiers fighting in the Crimea, she volunteered at once and left for Constantinople almost immediately. With her she took a small band of nurses.

Once in Turkey, she was given charge of the nursing at the military hospital. Even though doctors were hostile toward her and the hospital itself was deplorably filthy, she dug in her heels and began caring for her patients, at first using the provisions she had brought with her and then undertaking a correspondence campaign to resupply the hospital. She spent many hours each day in the wards, touching virtually every man who ever entered the hospital. The comfort she gave on night rounds earned her the nickname "The Lady with the Lamp." It was during those long days and nights, caring for the young British soldiers, that she developed a mother's love and began to call the ones she saved "my children."

On Florence Nightingale's return to England in the summer of 1856, near collapse from her war-time service, she discovered that she had become a national heroine and was honored with a brooch from Queen Victoria, which bore the words, "Blessed are the Merciful."

Queen Victoria also wrote, "You are, I know, well aware of the high sense I entertain of the Christian devotion which you have displayed during this great and bloody war, and I need hardly repeat to you how warm my admiration is for your services, which are fully equal to those of my dear and brave soldiers, whose sufferings you have had the privilege of alleviating in so merciful a manner. It will be a very great satisfaction to me to make the acquaintance of one who has set so bright an example of our sex."

Even though doctors had ordered bed rest for her, Florence went before Queen Victoria and Prince Albert to describe the deplorable medical conditions of the battlefield, which took as many lives as the enemy's bullets.

"You might as well take 1,100 men every year out upon Salisbury Plain and shoot them," Florence told them.

Impressed by her passionate plea for reform, the Queen remarked, "I wish we had her in the War Office." But women were not allowed to serve there.

Instead, in 1860 she opened the Nightingale Training School for Nurses at St. Thomas' Hospital. In addition, the hygiene reforms she suggested were adopted, and the mortality rate for the army was cut in half after the Crimean War.

Ill health plagued the final years of Florence Nightingale's life, but even from her bed, she worked with the British Army in India and was soon called the "Governess of the Governors of India."

Watching her mother show compassion for the poor, Florence learned the great satisfaction that comes from serving others. And even though her path of service diverged from her mother's wishes, she has earned the acclaim of a grateful world and become a spiritual mother to millions.

A Mother of Influence allows her children to answer God's call.

ALICE CHLOESY SULLIVAN

? - 1875

ANNE SULLIVAN MACY. Despite a lack of mothering from Alice Sullivan, teacher Anne Sullivan became like a mother to Helen Keller, and it was her love and devotion which finally broke through the silence and darkness of Helen's world.

⚬✖⚬

In the late nineteenth century, a young girl known as "Little Annie" Sullivan was locked in the dungeon of a mental institution outside Boston—the only place, said the doctors, for the hopelessly insane.

The first fourteen years of her life in poverty and abuse had left their mark. When Annie was just a baby, her mother, Alice, developed tuberculosis and died when she was only nine. Her alcoholic father, Thomas Sullivan, regularly beat the young girl to suppress her strong will. Finally, he abandoned his three children and took off for Chicago—never to be heard from again.

Annie had been partially blinded by an eye disease called trachoma, and her brother Jimmie had a tubercular tumor on his hip. Baby sister Mary was the only healthy one and was claimed by an aunt and uncle. But nobody wanted the two disabled children.

Without mother or father or anyone to claim them, Annie and Jimmie were sent to the infamous Tewksbury poorhouse in Massachusetts, a filthy place that served as a combination hospital, prison, and insane asylum—hell on earth for those who were kept there. Within a few months, her brother died, and Annie would be imprisoned there for four long years.

Annie was caged, and at times acted like the animal the staff had created, even attacking those who came near her. At other times, she sat in a daze.

One bright spot was an elderly nurse, who held hope for all God's children, and she began taking her lunch break in the dungeon, just outside Little Annie's cage. She hoped in some way to communicate love to her. One day she left her dessert—a brownie—where Annie could reach it. Annie showed no recognition of the kindness, but the next day, the nurse found the brownie had been eaten. Every Thursday thereafter, she brought a brownie to Annie.

As weeks passed, doctors noticed a change in Little Annie. After several months, they moved her upstairs. Doctors operated on her eyes and tried new treatments, but nothing seemed to help. It seemed to Annie that she would become a permanent resident in the horrid facility.

One day in 1880, several state officials made a tour of Tewksbury because of complaints and rumors about the appalling conditions. As the officials were about to leave, Annie literally threw herself at them, begging for a chance to leave and attend school. The head of the group was moved by her desperation and made it possible for her to attend the Perkins Institution for the Blind in Boston. After undergoing two more eye operations there, Annie was finally able to read.

After graduating from Perkins in 1886 with honors, Anne Sullivan was offered a job as a teacher for six-year-old Helen Keller—a blind, deaf, and mute child—who lived in Tuscumbia, Alabama. Anne was not quite twenty-one when she began work with Helen.

Because of her disabilities, Helen's parents had let her run wild, never punishing her for her actions. Anne persuaded them to allow her to move with Helen into a cottage on their large property, where she spent the next two weeks taming the wild child with love. Only a month after her arrival, Anne had taught Helen to recognize and spell the word "w-a-t-e-r."

"We walked down the path to the well-house," wrote Helen Keller about the incident. "Someone was drawing water and my teacher placed my hand under the spout. As the cool stream gushed over one hand she spelled into the other the word water, first slowly, then rapidly. Suddenly I felt a misty consciousness as of something forgotten—a thrill of returning thought. I knew then that "w-a-t-e-r" meant the wonderful cool something that was flowing over my hand. That living word awakened my soul."

In 1905, Anne married John Macy, an instructor at Harvard, who moved in with the two women, but the marriage was not a happy one, and they separated nine years later.

For fifty years, despite her own disabilities, Anne Sullivan devoted her life to Helen Keller, helping her through college and as she became a renowned world traveler and speaker. Although Helen started taking speech lessons in 1890, she could never speak clearly, and Anne would interpret for her.

> **CHOSEN BY GOD FOR THIS NEW LIFE OF LOVE, DRESS IN THE WARDROBE GOD PICKED OUT FOR YOU: COMPASSION, KINDNESS, HUMILITY, QUIET STRENGTH, DISCIPLINE.**
>
> COLOSSIANS 3:12 MSG

In a letter to a friend, Anne Sullivan Macy described how she helped Helen in her day-to-day life: "The genius is [Helen's], but much of the drudgery is mine. The difficulties under which she works are so insurmountable. Someone must always be at her side to read to her, to keep her typewriter in order, to read over her manuscript, make corrections, and look up words for her, and to do the many things which she would do for herself if she had her sight."

Because Anne's own eyes continued to deteriorate and she could read only a few hours a day with something called "double-lensed telescopic glasses," which were quite heavy, Polly Thomson, who had become a companion to both Anne and Helen, took over much of the traveling with Helen. One of Anne's last tasks before cataracts totally blinded her was to update Helen Keller's autobiography.

When Anne died of a heart problem on October 20, 1936, the New York Times told the story of how she had triumphed "over a dark and sordid environment and terrible poverty . . ." to bring "light to one in a double prison of darkness and silence and liberated her spirit. She deserves a place among the world's greatest teachers." Mark Twain called her a "miracle worker."

The kindness of one elderly nurse to "Little Annie" Sullivan rippled through history, influencing and inspiring the world.

A Mother of Influence extends kindness to all children.

GERTRUDE JENKINS JOHNSON WILLIAMS

Unknown

JOHN HAROLD JOHNSON. With hard work and determination, "Miss Gert" sought every opportunity possible to propel her son into becoming the most successful African-American publisher in history.

⌒∾⌒

One of the most vivid memories John H. Johnson has of his mother is of gripping her hand as they ran from the rampaging waters of a broken Mississippi River levee. The family lost everything, but "Miss Gert" was not a quitter. Born in poverty to former slaves in Lake Village, Arkansas, she had only a third-grade education, but she worked hard in the fields and kitchens of the Mississippi Valley. She had known little but backbreaking work all her life.

Later, she moved to Arkansas City, where she married Richard Lewis and had a daughter Beulah, but the marriage didn't last long. She then married Leroy Johnson, John's father, who worked as a laborer in the local sawmill and on the levee. His half-sister was fourteen when John was born in a tin-roofed shack.

There was little money in their household, but there was lots of love. John didn't know his father too well because he was always gone, traveling from one sawmill camp to another up and down the Mississippi River, but he knew his mother as a small, determined woman who didn't let anything stop her—not even the death of John's father, who was killed in a sawmill accident when the boy was only eight. Despite the few opportunities for blacks in those pre-Depression days, "Miss Gert" clung to a dream that her son would one day become "somebody."

Next she married James Williams, a delivery man for the local bakery. To supplement the family income, John and his mother both worked. She ran field kitchens for a dredging company, as well as doing personal laundry for the crew. John helped by washing and ironing clothes when he was still a young boy.

ALL HARD WORK BRINGS A PROFIT.

PROVERBS 14:23 NIV

"Miss Gert" was saving every penny she could to move the family to Chicago, where she thought there would be better schools and opportunity for John. But when he finished the eighth grade, she still didn't have enough money to make it happen. There was no high school in Arkansas City for John to attend, so she made him repeat eighth grade and said she would make him do it as many years as she had to rather than let him run wild or do hard labor like his father.

John Johnson later wrote that the neighbors thought his mother "was crazy for making sacrifices for a boy who would never amount to anything anyway." He had three strikes against him already: the Great Depression, his race, and living in the South.

But save she did, and when she had enough money to head north to Chicago, she and John left and moved into the same apartment house where her older daughter, Beulah, rented a room. "Miss Gert" went to work as a domestic and then worked in the garment industry. His stepfather had stayed in Arkansas but joined them soon after. By 1934 "Miss Gert" had lost her job, and John's stepfather couldn't find work, so for the next two years they subsisted on public relief funds.

When John entered nearly all-black Wendell Phillips High School in the fall of 1933, he skipped ninth grade and entered the tenth. Repeating the eight grade had not hurt him at all. By this time, he had decided that he wanted to be a journalist, so during high school he edited the school newspaper and was the yearbook sales manager. He was also the junior and senior class president, presiding officer of the student council, and leader of the student forum and French club.

But they were still poor in Chicago — no money for bus fare — and he remembers walking to school in the bitter cold. His first year, he was teased mercilessly by his classmates for his hick accent, bowlegs, and clothes homemade by his mother. When John came home crying, "Miss Gert" persuaded the woman she still worked for in the garment district to give her some old suits outgrown by the woman's son. John became the best-dressed kid in school!

Reading was his passion, and he haunted the local library, even checking out self-improvement books by such notables as Dale Carnegie. In his autobiography, *Succeeding Against the Odds*, John wrote, "Faith, self-confidence, and a positive mental attitude: These three were the basic messages of the self-help books that changed my life." With the backing of his supportive mother, John would stand in front of the mirror at home, practicing his speeches and introducing himself to girls.

John graduated with honors and received a tuition scholarship to the University of Chicago. His mother had proved to him how hard work, determination, and persistence could help him succeed.

Harry H. Pace, president of the black-owned Supreme Life Insurance Company of America, gave John his first part-time job in the city. One of his first duties was to browse through magazines and find articles of interest to reprint in the company newsletter that was sent to clients.

When twenty-four-year-old John had an idea for his first magazine, modeled after the success of *Reader's Digest*, and could not obtain financing from white bankers, his mother came to his aid. They used her new furniture as collateral for a start-up loan. After *Negro Digest* became a success, John was able to do what he had dreamed about for years: he "retired" his mother, putting her on his personal payroll.

For fifty-nine years, John saw or talked to his mother almost every day. Even when he found himself in other nations, he called his mother daily—once, from atop a telephone pole in Haiti. He continued to draw upon her spiritual and physical toughness until she died. John went on to publish *Ebony* and *Jet* magazines, and his company owns three radio stations. He says, "Not a day passes that I don't feed off the bread of her spirit."

A Mother of Influence teaches her children the value of perseverance.

ELIZA DAVISON ROCKEFELLER

1813 - 1889

JOHN D. ROCKEFELLER. A devout Christian, Eliza Rockefeller

engrained a sense of responsibility for others in her son, who

became one of the greatest philanthropists of all time.

◦◦✦◦◦

Born of Scottish stock, Eliza Davison Rockefeller was an intelligent
woman with highly developed common sense. A straitlaced disciplinarian, she was devoutly religious and a believer in hard work
and thrift. Her strong will and deep piety gave her a remarkable serenity,
which she passed on to her son, John D. Rockefeller, who was born July
8, 1839, in Richford, New York. She made sure that John and his five
brothers and sisters were trained in matters of holiness, orderliness, and
industry. Weekly attendance at church and Sunday school was mandato-
ry.

In contrast, John's father, William Avery Rockefeller, exuded a joy of
life and loved music and social conversation. While his mother imbued
her son with faith, his farmer father, who traded in commodities like salt
and timber, taught him to recognize and develop his innate gift for business. Selling turkeys to their neighbors at the age of seven was John's
first foray into commerce. Both Eliza and William alike were concerned
that all their children grow up self-reliant, honest, keen-witted, and
dependable.

Later in life, John recalled that both of his parents were examples of
politeness and patience. He said, "I cannot remember to have heard the
voices of either Father or Mother raised in anger or complaint in speaking

to any of us."

Eliza and William also instilled in their son a rich heritage of giving to church and charities, the gifts being made from their childhood earnings.

When John was eleven, the family moved to Oswego, New York, where he attended an academy with excellent teachers. "I was not an easy student," he wrote, but because he was a diligent and serious student, John excelled at school.

In 1853, the family moved again to Cleveland, Ohio, but here, John was able to attend Cleveland High School, again distinguishing himself as a good student, especially in mathematics. At the age of sixteen, he graduated.

By this time, his father had left farming and gone into the patent herbal medicine business, often making itinerant sales trips out West. William encouraged his son to go into business, although as a serious student John D. Rockefeller might well have preferred to go to college. But following his father's advice, he enrolled in a three-month bookkeeping course at Folsom's Commercial College.

Already showing his gift for shrewd business acumen, Rockefeller began looking for a job in Cleveland, but only at the largest firms where he could be trained in greater things. The amount of salary was no object.

"I did not guess what it would be," Rockefeller once said, "but I was after something big."

His first job with a group of commission merchants, who did business with wholesale and retail businesses, as well as railroads and steamship lines, earned him $3.50 a week.

Because his mother had set an example of church attendance, Rockefeller became a member of Erie Street Baptist Church in 1854, quickly becoming an important layman. He would do anything for the small congregation, from washing windows to sweeping floors, to serving as its clerk, raising money for a Sunday school library, and finally becoming one of the church's five trustees. From the beginning, he tithed to the church, giving one-tenth of his tiny salary. As a supporter of abolition, he once gave more than a tenth of his earnings to help a Negro man in Cincinnati buy his slave wife.

During the three and a half years Rockefeller worked for others, he earned the respect of bankers and businessmen, and afterward became a partner with Maurice B. Clark to handle a variety of goods—grain, hay, meats, and miscellaneous commodities. With $4,000 between them, the pair grossed more than $450,000 that first year and made a $4,400 profit.

With the onset of the Civil War, their business boomed, as they supplied the army, industry, and shipped food products to Europe.

In the meantime, he married Laura Celestia Spelman, the daughter of a Cleveland businessman, and they eventually had four children, who grew up to become one of the leading industrial and philanthropic families in America.

> **DO NOT WITHHOLD GOOD FROM THOSE WHO DESERVE IT, WHEN IT IS IN YOUR POWER TO ACT.**
> PROVERBS 3:27 NIV

With the huge profits he made during wartime, Rockefeller plunged into the new oil industry and quickly gained a monopoly, bringing stability to a chaotic business atmosphere. This was possible because at the time, there were no antimonopoly laws, so Rockefeller owned the oil from the wellhead to the refinery, paid no income tax, and did not have to worry about huge shipping charges since there was no railroad rate regulation. Plus, the gasoline-powered automobile began to roll out, increasing the demand for his product. In addition, because his mother passed on to him her traits of frugality, attention to detail, and an intolerance for waste, Rockefeller became fabulously wealthy.

With his wealth, he believed, came a public obligation to give to worthy causes—schools, hospitals, libraries, colleges, churches, asylums, foreign missions, and temperance. That sense of public obligation was passed down through the next generations as well, and his descendants carry on his legacy of giving.

At one point, Rockefeller's wealth was estimated to be as much as $900,000,000 and he is considered to be one of the most outstanding philanthropists of all time, giving away as much as a half billion dollars in his lifetime. With the creation of the Rockefeller Foundation in 1913, his influence is still felt through its generous giving today.

But more importantly, Eliza and her husband, William, gave their son, John D. Rockefeller, a happy childhood—a gift he valued throughout his life far more than the millions of dollars he made.

A Mother of Influence makes thrift a part of her children's education.

MARY REDDIN LIDDELL

Unknown

ERIC HENRY LIDDELL. As a living example, Mary Liddell

had modeled for her athletic, missionary son total trust and

complete commitment to Christ.

⚜

The start gun popped, and the race was on. Runners from all over the world had come to the 1924 Paris Olympics for this one moment—the four-hundred-meter race. The crowd in the stands cheered wildly as the runners, with perfect form, approached the finish line.

Then out from the group burst a lone runner, head thrown back, face to the sky, and arms waving like windmills, causing him to wobble as he ran. A new roar went up from the crowd. They had been waiting for this famous Scotsman, Eric Liddell, to lunge into his famous "complete surrender" run. They knew that when Eric's head flew back and he let go, he was going to win.

Eric didn't even know until he crossed the finish line where he was on the track or where the other runners were. Many have said that the way Eric ran was a small example of the way he lived his life. He was utterly and completely surrendered to God.

How could Eric live this way? How could he trust God so much that he let go of his grasp on the race and his own life? His parents had also been people of faith who surrendered wholeheartedly as missionaries to China during a time when it meant danger and the possible sacrifice of their own lives.

Eric's mother, Mary Reddin, was born in Paxton, Scotland, and grew into a quiet gentle woman with dark brown hair worn in a bun. She became a nurse and worked at a hospital in Glasgow. When Mary became ill, she went to stay with some friends in the seaside resort of Stirling to recuperate. While there, she attended a church picnic where she met James Dunlop Liddell, a warm-hearted, peaceful man who had left his job as a drapery maker to become a missionary. They fell in love and were engaged soon afterward.

> WE HAVE THIS TREASURE IN EARTHEN VESSELS, SO THAT THE SURPASSING GREATNESS OF THE POWER WILL BE OF GOD AND NOT FROM OURSELVES."
>
> 2 CORINTHIANS 4:7 NASB

Their engagement came quickly, but their marriage would be delayed for another six years. During this time they were separated frequently. James attended a Congregational college in Glasgow, completing his coursework before being ordained for the mission field. Meanwhile, Mary patiently kept working as a nurse. In 1898 James was accepted by the London Missionary Society and given a mission station in Mongolia (Northern China). It seemed like the right time to marry, but James would have to prove himself out in the field before the Missionary Society would send Mary to him.

Still a single woman, she took a nursing job in the Outer Hebrides, tending to the cuts and wounds of the young women who worked on the docks cleaning fish that came in from the three hundred boats in the area. This is where she developed her own system of "instant first aid" that she would later need in China. Finally, on October 23, 1899, Miss Reddin landed in Shanghai and married her beloved Mr. Liddell.

At that time, China boiled with rebellion and anger. More than two hundred Western missionaries were massacred along with thirty thousand Chinese Christians by a group called "The Boxers," who vowed to rid China of all Westerners. It was an atmosphere that would forge the Liddell's amazing character traits—those they would pass on to their children.

As the persecution worsened, the Liddells were forced to flee to the London Missionary Society compound in Shanghai, leaving all their belongings behind. During the next few years, the Liddells would go into China and then out to safer mission compounds in Shanghai and Tientsin when the danger rose. During this time of uncertainty, their first child, Robert Victor, was born. Then later, Eric Henry.

Mary had given birth to Eric during one of those times when she was safely tucked away in one of the missionary compounds, while her husband worked on the mission field. She could have packed up her children and gone home to Scotland at this point, and no one would have blamed her. A lot of missionaries were doing that very thing. Yet, because she felt so strongly that she was to serve with her husband as a missionary and because of her absolute trust in God and complete surrender to His will, she took her children back on the field. Undaunted, she set out on a two-day journey by train, followed by a forty-mile ride in an old cart over bumpy roads, to work side by side with her husband.

They made it through the next nine hard years, living in humble surroundings and doing without a lot of things they could have had back in Scotland. Their son Ernest and their first daughter, Jenny, were born during this time. Finally, in 1907, the Liddell family went home on their first furlough.

Eric and his brother attended an all-boys' school where Eric excelled in sports-especially running. He won so many trophies that his mother had trouble finding places to put them. His parents were thrilled. Later Eric attended Edinburgh University, where he qualified for the 1924 Paris Olympics. But when one of his races was scheduled to be run on the Sabbath, he refused to participate, causing quite a controversy, which is portrayed in the movie *Chariots of Fire*. By being obedient to God and running another event on a different day, he went back to Scotland with a gold medal.

Eric also made the decision—without doubt or reservation—to return to China as a missionary. He simply knew he was meant to go back. He married Florence Mackenzie, who joined him in China, and they had three daughters.

The end of Eric's life was like looking through a magnifying glass at what he had always been. In 1941, Eric was separated from his wife and children and sent to a Japanese internment camp, along with many other foreigners from countries all over the world.

With limited equipment and living among the rats and open sewage, Eric gave himself completely to others as he had always done throughout his life. He knew and encouraged everyone, winning their respect and love. He organized races, hockey games, basketball, soccer, and rounders for the children. He became Uncle Eric to those children, many of whom had not seen their own parents in years. The elderly and the sick would never have made it without his sparkling blue eyes and encouraging smile. He even taught science classes and preached sermons. Many said that he was a true example of Christ.

It came as a shock to the other prisoners when Eric died on February 21, 1945. He had suffered much from a brain tumor, but he had never revealed his pain to the others. Everyone in the camp attended his funeral, and he was buried in the little cemetery there. One man who had been a child at the time said, "None of us will ever forget this man who was totally committed to putting God first."

Eric had learned total trust and complete commitment to Christ from his mother Mary's living example. His deep relationship with Christ helped him to keep trusting the Lord even when his world was at its darkest. Five months after his death, the camp was liberated by American airmen. It seems a tragic ending to a heroic story, but Eric had already been liberated. He was now with Christ, the One he loved most.

A Mother of Influence becomes a living example of Christ to her children.

CAROLYN WESTON McWILLIAMS

Unknown

JULIA CHILD. Because Carolyn McWilliams was such a

fun-loving mother, eldest daughter Julia Child's

adventurous life sprang from a happy childhood.

⌘

Women are often tempted to think that their homemaking skills are what make a house a home, but the mother of one of the most famous chefs of all times, Julia Child, rarely cooked!
Born into affluence in Pasadena, California, in 1912, Julia, along with her sister, Dorothy, and brother, John, lived in relative comfort, taken care of by servants and a cook. They all attended private schools. Their mother, Carolyn McWilliams, depended on the cook to prepare "good plain New England food," Julia Child once said in an interview with *People* magazine. "We always had a soup course, meat, and vegetables. Things like roast beef and leg of lamb—with roast potatoes and mint sauce." The basics were supplemented with abundant fresh fruits and vegetables from the bountiful Southern California farms nearby.

As a child, and later as the star of eight different television cooking shows, Julia was known for her good-natured humor and ability to laugh at herself—qualities passed on to her by her mother.

"I know I'm happy," Julia once said. "I was very fortunate in my family background because I had a very loving, supportive family. We had no conflict. My sister was five years younger and we had a brother halfway between, so we never had any sibling rivalry. My parents were happy; we were not rich, but comfortably well-off. My mother thought everything we did was absolutely marvelous.

"I think your background makes an awful lot of difference. I don't know what you do if you've been abused, or haven't been praised enough so that you don't feel that you're okay. I was very fortunate in having such a happy background. I was never brilliant in school, but I never had any problems either, so I didn't feel inferior. I did have the problem of being twice as tall as anyone else, but that didn't seem to make any difference because my mother always said we were so wonderful, no matter what."

> **BETTER A DRY CRUST WITH PEACE AND QUIET THAN A HOUSE FULL OF FEASTING, WITH STRIFE.**
>
> PROVERBS 17:1 NIV

All of the unusually tall McWilliams children were athletic and loved playing outdoor games and sports. In those days, it was safe to roam their Pasadena neighborhood with a group of friends, climbing trees and enjoying the almost year-round perfect weather.

By her early teen years, Julia felt like a giant at six-feet, two-inches. Thin and limber, the future chef excelled at tennis, skiing, and many other sports. But wanting her to obtain even better instruction, at the end of her ninth grade year, the young girl was sent to the Katherine Branson School for Girls in Northern California, where she quickly became the social leader. According to her biographer Noël Riley Fitch, Julia became known for "her commanding physical presence, her verbal openness, and her physical pranks and adventure."

Since the school was near San Francisco, on Saturdays Julia and her friends would "put on our Prince Matchabelli cherry-red lipstick . . . and have artichokes and cinnamon toast," she told the New York Times. "We thought we were so elegant."

After graduation in 1930, Julia Child went to Smith College in Massachusetts and majored in history. But she also considered life as a novelist, or perhaps a basketball player, since she was so tall and athletic. It was all a dream, because "Middle-class women did not have careers," she said. "You were to marry and have children and be a nice mother. You didn't go out and do anything." So after graduation, Julia returned to home in Pasadena.

She soon grew restless and went back East to New York, where she shared an apartment with Smith classmates and worked for the advertising manager of Sloane's, a prestigious home-furnishings company. But she would only stay a few years. Worried about her mother's failing health, she went home to Pasadena, and Carolyn McWilliams died just two months later.

For a while, Julia stayed home to take care of her dad, John, a community leader and businessman, but when World War II broke out in 1941, Julia wanted to do something useful for the war effort. She tried to join the WACS or the WAVES, but was rejected because of her height.

Instead, she went to work for the Office of Strategic Services (O.S.S.) in Washington, D.C., the forerunner of the Central Intelligence Agency, hoping to work as a spy in exotic places. Wearing army fatigues, Julia was sent overseas . . . as a clerk. It wasn't terribly glamorous working as a clerk on troop ships and sleeping on cots.

In 1943, Julia McWilliams met the love of her life, Paul Cushing Child of Boston, while they were both stationed in Ceylon (now Sri Lanka). A sophisticated artist, Paul worked as a map- and chart-maker. At forty-one, he was ten years older than she, but she was several inches taller. The attraction was instant, and when they were both assigned to duty in China, their romance deepened. In the early days, it was Paul, not Julia, who was the gourmet.

After the war in 1946, Julia and Paul were married and moved to Washington, D.C., where he became a member of the Foreign Service. Through the years, they traveled all over the world as he was posted to various countries.

While living in France, Julia studied French and enrolled for a six-month course at the Cordon Bleu Cooking School in Paris, the first American woman who had ever done so. There she met two of her future book collaborators, Simone Beck and Louisette Bertholle, who were working on a French cookbook for American women. When *Mastering the Art of French Cooking* was published in the early sixties, it became a best-seller.

When her husband, Paul, retired in the early sixties, they settled in Cambridge, Massachusetts, and Julia Child hit the airwaves with the first of her cooking shows. Its appeal was Julia's "charm, lack of pretension and endearing klutziness," a *Time* magazine writer said. "What keeps her fans turning on her TV show is the same thing that sent their parents to the movie theaters to watch *The Perils of Pauline*: suspense. For from the moment that Julia appears on the screen, sleeves rolled above the elbow and blue denim apron about her waist, until her closing 'Bon appetit,' there is no telling what calamity may confront her."

Because of the show's low budget, there were no retakes. If Julia splattered an egg on the floor, or a turkey skidded across the counter, viewers experienced it all.

When Paul Child suffered a series of strokes, beginning in 1989, he was moved to a Cambridge nursing home. Until his death in 1994, Julia visited her husband every day, as well as frequently speaking to him on the phone. When he died, she thought her life was over, too, and that she would never write again.

But master chef Julia Child continued to write and appear on television well into her eighties. In 2000, the French awarded her the Legion d'Honneur, their most prestigious honor. Her famous kitchen was dismantled and reassembled at the Museum of American History at the Smithsonian Institution, and in July of 2003, she received the Presidential Medal of Freedom.

When she died on August 13, 2004, at her home in Santa Barbara at the age of ninety-one, the qualities passed on to her by her mother were still in evidence: her signature cheery smile, her endearing charm, and her enthusiasm for life.

A Mother of Influence has fun with her children.

LENNIS "LYNNE" WASHINGTON

Unknown

DENZEL WASHINGTON. According to her famous

actor son, Denzel Washington, Lynne kept him

on the straight and narrow and is responsible for

his phenomenal success as an actor.

⚭

In speaking of his mother Lynne to the Washington Post, Denzel Washington recalled, "She was very, very tough, a tough disciplinarian. Even when I was 15 or 16, I had to be home by the time the street lights went on. She saw to it I was exposed to a lot of things. She couldn't afford it, but she was very intelligent. She is basically responsible for my success."

Blessed with good looks and intelligence, Denzel was born on December 28, 1954, in Mount Vernon, New York, to his mother, Lynne, a beautician and former gospel singer, and his father, Denzel, a Pentecostal minister. In their middle-class neighborhood, bordering the Bronx, Denzel's friends came in all colors—West Indians, Blacks, Irish, Italians—which would serve as a rich background for his future acting career.

But acting wasn't on the Washington agenda. "My father was down on the movies," Denzel told the *Chicago Tribune*, "and his idea of something worthwhile would be *The King of Kings*, *The Ten Commandments*, and *101 Dalmatians*. And I knew no actors. It's a wonder I ever went into acting."

But it was his mother's firm hand that guided her son Denzel, his older sister Lorice, and younger brother, David. By grounding them in solid values and encouraging participation in organizations like the Boys Club and the Young Men's Christian Association (YMCA), Lynne was a great influence on her children. Plus she taught Denzel a work ethic. When he was only twelve, he worked part-time in the barbershop his mother co-owned, brushing hair off the clothes of clients.

Because they lived in a more affluent neighborhood and were sheltered by their parents, Denzel and his siblings knew little about the Civil Rights Movement, and the rhetoric of men like Malcolm X was kept from their tender ears.

"We just didn't listen to that kind of talk in my father's house," he told the *New York Times Magazine*. "Most of the talk around the house was about the Bible. It wasn't that [talk of racism] was forbidden."

At the age of fourteen, the world as Denzel knew it came crashing down around him. His mother and father divorced. In retaliation, he rejected his religion and became disobedient at home and at school. It hurt—badly. Although he is now on friendly terms with both parents, he told the *Washington Post* that when he was a young teen, "I guess it made me angry. I went through a phase where I got into a lot of fights. Working it out, you know."

His high school guidance counselor suggested to his mother that Denzel apply to a private boarding school—Oakland Academy—in upstate New York, which boasted a wealthy white student body. Much to his surprise, Denzel was accepted and granted a full scholarship. There he excelled in all sports—football, basketball, track, and baseball. He also joined a local black band called the Last Express as their piano man.

After graduating from Oakland, he entered Fordham University in the Bronx as a pre-med major. Money was tight, and he paid for college with several loans and ran an after-school baby-sitting service at a Greek Orthodox Church in Upper Manhattan. One semester, he was forced to drop out of school because of poor grades and first worked at the post office and then as a trash collector. Realizing he wanted more out of life, Denzel quickly returned to Fordham.

> LET YOUR EYES LOOK RIGHT ON [WITH FIXED PURPOSE], AND LET YOUR GAZE BE STRAIGHT BEFORE YOU. CONSIDER WELL THE PATH OF YOUR FEET, AND LET ALL YOUR WAYS BE ESTABLISHED AND ORDERED ARIGHT.
>
> PROVERBS 4:25-26 AMP

While serving as a YMCA camp counselor one summer, he told the *Chicago Tribune* that "I organized a talent show, and someone told me, 'You seem real natural on the stage; did you ever think of becoming an actor?' Bing! That's all it took."

That fall, he won the lead role in Eugene O'Neill's *The Emperor Jones*, over a number of theater majors. He starred in several other productions, but Shakespeare's *Othello* was his showcase role. Denzel's drama instructor at the time was Robinson Stone, a retired actor, who told the *Chicago Tribune*, "He was thrilling even then. He was easily the best Othello I had ever seen, and I had seen Paul Robeson play it. He played Othello with so much majesty and beauty but also rage and hate that I dragged agents to come and see it."

After being contacted by an agent, Denzel—even though he was still in school—was offered a small role in *Wilma*, a TV drama about the runner Wilma Rudolph. He then studied acting for a time at the American Conservatory Theater in San Francisco before heading to Los Angeles to break into show business. When his first attempt was unsuccessful, Denzel returned to his mother's house in Mount Vernon.

Later, while attending a play, he saw Pauletta Pearson, whom he had met during the filming of *Wilma*, and she eventually moved into Lynne's house. The couple later married, and she became his encouragement during the hard times when Denzel was trying to break into acting.

After he played Dr. Phillip Chandler in the TV drama *St. Elsewhere* for five years, Hollywood began to realize his incredible talent and potential. Denzel went on to win an Academy Award for best supporting actor in 1990 for his character of Trip in the Civil War film *Glory*, and in 2002, he won the Academy Award for best actor in a lead role in *Training Day*. In the Academy's seventy-three-year history, Denzel Washington was only the second African-American actor—Sidney Poitier was the first—to win an Oscar for best actor in a lead role.

While acting is his gift, Denzel considers his wife, Pauletta, and their four children as the most important part of his life. He's very much a family man and carpools just like other dads. If possible, every movie contract he signs has a special clause that allows him to fly home to Beverly Hills on weekends to see his family. He told a Washington Post reporter that "Acting is just a way of making a living. Family is life. When you experience a child, you know that's life."

The faith he inherited from his mother is a vital part of his personality as well. During a 1995 visit to Africa, Denzel and Pauletta renewed their wedding vows in a ceremony conducted by Archbishop Desmond Tutu. He has said that it's important to him and his wife to model a healthy family life in Hollywood.

As a young teen, divorce could have ended a promising career for Denzel Washington before it even began. Thanks to his mother's influence, Denzel is fulfilling his life's work.

A Mother of Influence keeps her children on the straight and narrow.

NANCY WALTON

Unknown

SAM WALTON. Sam Walton's mother, Nan, kept the "home fires" burning, providing a stable environment for the man who would become the founder of retail giant Wal-Mart.

⌘

When Nan Walton's husband, Thomas, moved his family from Kingfisher, Oklahoma, where Sam was born on March 29, 1918, to several rural communities in his native Missouri, she was always there for her husband and children, doing what was necessary to keep the "home fires" burning.

Sam's father, a farm-mortgage banker, believed in the concept of saving, so when the bottom dropped out during the Great Depression, the family suffered less than most of their neighbors, although they had to pinch pennies.

"We never thought of ourselves as poor," Sam Walton wrote in his autobiography, *Made in America*, "although we certainly didn't have much of what you'd call disposable income lying around, and we did what we could to raise a dollar here and there. For example, my mother, Nan Walton, got the idea during the Depression to start a little milk business. I'd get up early in the morning and milk the cows, Mother would prepare and bottle the milk, and I'd deliver it after football practice in the afternoons. We had ten or twelve customers, who paid ten cents a gallon. Best of all, Mother would skim the cream and make ice cream, and it's a wonder I wasn't known as Fat Sam Walton in those days from all the ice cream I ate."

Nan had finished a year of college before she married Thomas Walton and, according to Walton, his mother's greatest desire was for her family to get a higher education.

Walton described his mother as "extremely ambitious" for her kids and encouraged them to read and pursue education, even though she had little herself. He went on to say, "Mother must have been a pretty special motivator, because I took her seriously when she told me I should always try to be the best I could at whatever I took on. So, I have always pursued everything I was interested in with a true passion—some would say obsession—to win."

Because of his mother's influence, even at an early age, the good-humored Sam was ambitious. At the age of thirteen, living first in Marshall and then Shelbina, Missouri, he became the youngest ever in the state of Missouri at that time to attain the rank of Eagle Scout.

But it would be in Columbia, home of the University of Missouri, where Sam Walton would shine in every activity he tackled. At Hickman High School in Columbia, he played quarterback for the football team, was captain of the basketball team, and led the school as class president and student council president. In 1936 the Hickman yearbook named him Most Versatile Boy, and the description beneath his picture read that he had received the award for "leadership, service, and ability."

Sam Walton was not afraid of hard work. Throughout his college years, the young student financed his education with a paper route, graduating in 1940 with a degree in economics. But he was still unsure of his life's career. Since economics had been his major, he finally decided to take a job as a sales trainee with a J.C. Penney retail store in Des Moines, Iowa. When Penney was still alive, the older man would pay surprise visits to his stores across the country, and one day Sam met the retailing legend.

"He taught me to tie a package with very little twine and very little paper and still make it look nice," Sam Walton said. He had learned one of the most important lessons that would guide him in the founding of his Wal-Mart empire: give the customer good service and quality merchandise, but keep the margins low.

Walton might have stayed at Penney's, but a war was raging in Europe and in the Pacific. In 1942 he was drafted into the Army Intelligence Corps as a communications officer, which kept him in the States for the duration of World War II. A year later, he married Helen

LORD, THROUGH ALL THE GENERATIONS YOU HAVE BEEN OUR HOME!

PSALM 90:1 NLT

Robson and had four children.

After his service in the army, Walton was eager to get back to work, but he had no interest in making money for someone else. In 1945 he and his brother James borrowed $45,000, a big sum in those days, and leased a retail space in Newport, Arkansas, to open a Ben Franklin five-and-dime store. Five years later, they shifted the operation to Bentonville, Arkansas, still the current home of the Wal-Mart corporation.

Always a practical visionary, Walton studied retail giants like K-Mart, accurately deciding that the small five-and-dime store was declining, and the future lay in big chain stores. But K-Mart and others like it avoided small towns, and the brothers surmised that if they started a chain to concentrate on more rural areas, they would be successful.

"There was a lot more business in those towns than people ever thought," Walton said in an interview.

Wal-Mart's philosophy has never changed from the beginning, when Sam Walton opened the first store to sell name-brand merchandise at low prices, while retaining a friendly general-store character. It was the right idea, at the right time, in the right place.

By the time Walton took the company public in 1970, there were about 25 Wal-Mart stores, and within two years, the chain had doubled to 64 stores with sales of $125 million. The stores were growing by leaps and bounds at this point, and in 1981 the company ballooned to 161 stores. Wal-Mart was the eighth largest retailer in America by 1983 with 642 stores and yearly sales figures of $4.2 billion. That same year *Forbes* magazine estimated Walton's net worth at $2.1 billion and ranked him as the second richest man in the United States. The retailing genius also opened the first wholesale Sam's Club that year.

The secret of his success, he told the *New York Times*, was simple. "Anyone willing to work hard, study the business, and apply the best principles can do well," he said. Walton must have been right. For more than a decade, his stores averaged more than 35 percent growth each year.

But being a conservative and thrifty employer, Sam Walton paid his employees minimum wage in the early days. It was his wife, Helen, who convinced him to share the wealth, giving incentive bonuses, merchandise discounts, and profit-sharing. The Wal-Mart corporation has been a good community partner for Bentonville as well. They built a senior citizens' recreation center, a library, day-care center, tennis courts, and a health club there, and the company regularly gives college scholarships to deserving students.

From his childhood, church participation was important to Sam Walton, and he faithfully served his local church. Some employees and townspeople called him "Mr. Sam," because he was so unpretentious. Despite his wealth, Sam Walton drove around town in a pickup truck, with cages for his hunting dogs in back.

When he died of bone cancer in 1992, shortly after receiving the Presidential Medal of Honor from the first President George Bush, his heirs received more than $23 billion in Wal-Mart stock. The corporation was worth $104.8 billion, had 2,300 stores five years after his death, and by 1999 had grown to 3,800 stores around the country.

Nan Walton never lived to see her son's phenomenal success. "One of the great sadnesses in my life is that she died young, of cancer," he wrote in *Made in America*, "just as we were beginning to do well in business."

But thanks to the solid foundation of his mother's love and her ambitions for him to excel, Sam Walton's retailing legacy continues to grow with no sign of slowing.

A Mother of Influence makes herself available to her children.

ELIZABETH MEYER GLASER

1947-1994

An AIDS activist until her death, Elizabeth Glaser

fought for medications and funding for pediatric AIDS victims

to help her children Ariel and Jake battle the deadly disease.

From the time Elizabeth Glaser gave birth to her beautiful baby girl Ariel in 1981, things went terribly wrong. It had been a difficult pregnancy, and Ariel was delivered by Caesarean section. Afterward, Elizabeth began to hemorrhage so severely that nurses quickly started a transfusion of seven pints of blood—blood unknowingly contaminated by the HIV virus.

Until then, Elizabeth considered her life to be blessed. She was born in 1947 to New York City businessman Max Meyer and his wife, Edith, an urban planner. She grew up in an upper middle-class neighborhood on Long Island and received her bachelor's degree at the University of Wisconsin and a master's degree in early childhood education at Boston University.

Even though she had a failed first marriage, she found satisfying work as a Head Start teacher in Denver but later moved to Los Angeles to teach and eventually was named director of programs at the Children's Museum there.

Writing in her 1991 book titled *Absence of Angels*, Elizabeth Meyer Glaser talked about meeting her husband, Paul Michael Glaser, an actor who was ready to explode on the scene with the *Starsky and Hutch* TV series. Stopping for a red light on Santa Monica Boulevard, she said she glanced over at the car beside her at "the cutest guy I have ever seen." He noticed her, too, jumped out of his car, and introduced himself. They were married in August of 1980.

> DEAR CHILDREN, LET US NOT LOVE WITH WORDS OR TONGUE BUT WITH ACTIONS AND IN TRUTH.
>
> 1 JOHN 3:18 NIV

Despite Elizabeth's risky birth experience, the couple never suspected there was anything wrong. When Elizabeth read a newspaper article a few weeks later, which said that the blood supply had been contaminated with HIV, she panicked and called her doctor. He assured her there was nothing to worry about.

Life was exceptionally good as Paul's career blossomed. They welcomed their son, Jake, into the family in 1984, and Elizabeth looked forward to having more children.

The Glasers were happy until 1986, when four-year-old Ariel began to suffer from baffling stomach pains, diarrhea, and draining fatigue. She underwent a battery of tests, which showed low T-cell counts, an indication that her immune system was not working properly. The tests for lupus and leukemia came back negative, but then the doctor suggested testing for AIDS. Their lives shattered like the colored pieces of a kaleidoscope when the test came back positive. How could this terrible thing happen to them?

They were even more shocked when further testing showed that both Elizabeth and their one-and-a-half-year-old son, Jake, were also infected with the virus. Doctors explained that Elizabeth probably contracted the disease from her transfusion, and then passed on the virus to Ariel during breast-feeding. Jake contracted the disease in the womb.

"In our worst nightmares," Elizabeth later wrote, "we could never have imagined the devastation of those few days. Our entire world had been crushed. It was too much to comprehend."

Their shock soon turned to rage when they realized how little was known about the disease in young children. Prior to that time, most cases of AIDS had been diagnosed in promiscuous homosexuals or drug users. But now its evil had touched a normal, happy family. If it could happen to them, it could happen to anyone.

Unfortunately, they had to hide the tragedy behind a wall of silence. Doctors advised them not to tell anyone about the diagnosis because of harassment that other AIDS victims had suffered. Only their closest family and friends, as well as a few others they felt ought to know, were told. In those days, people didn't know if it was easy or hard to transmit the disease to others. Some parents no longer allowed their children to play with Ariel and Jake, Elizabeth was asked to leave her yoga class, many psychiatrists refused to treat Ariel, and her daughter was even banned from the private school she attended.

When Ariel was seven, doctors told the Glasers to prepare for the worst. Their daughter's fate no longer loomed in the future; they were staring the certainty of death in the face.

Elizabeth said that she "could no longer sit quietly in Santa Monica. I had to do more." After Ariel's death on August 12, 1988, Elizabeth realized Jake's life hung in the balance, and she would have to fight for new drugs to save his life and educate people about the effect of AIDS on children.

"I wasn't trying to make people care about AIDS because it happened to my family," she later said. "I was just trying to make people care."

Elizabeth became a leading AIDS activist, cofounding the Pediatric AIDS Foundation in 1988. Many considered her the most effective AIDS lobbyist in the nation.

In 1989, when the Glasers found out a supermarket tabloid was going to publish a distorted story about their AIDS nightmare, they finally revealed their well-kept secret to the public. Amazingly, once all their friends and colleagues knew their story, many of them rallied to help.

Soon after, Elizabeth Glaser published *An Absence of Angels*, a book to give courage and hope to victims and to educate the public about pediatric AIDS. The title came from Elizabeth's realization that God was not going to intervene miraculously by taking the disease away, but rather that she would be empowered to help save herself and others from the terrible disease.

"It was Ari who taught me to love when all I wanted to do was hate," Elizabeth said. "She taught me to be brave when all I felt was fear. And she taught me to help others when all I wanted to do was help myself. I am active in fighting AIDS because I want to be a person she would be proud of; I was so proud of her. I think about her courage and I am able to go on."

Despite Elizabeth's declining health, she continued to travel and raise funds to fight pediatric AIDS and received visits by such notables as

Princess Diana.

Finally, on November 27, 1994, her husband, Paul, lit a menorah candle and sang Ma'oztur in observation of the first night of Hanukkah. Elizabeth was still alert that night, but would soon pass away on December 3. She was buried next to her daughter, Ariel, outside of Boston, a heroine to her family and to those who still fight against AIDS.

A Mother of Influence leads
her children to take action in their faith.

MINNIE ELIZABETH BOURKE-WHITE

Unknown

MARGARET BOURKE-WHITE. Perfectionist mother Minnie

White instilled in her daughter a sense that she was wanted and loved as

a female, and as a result, Margaret Bourke-White became one of

the most celebrated photojournalists of the twentieth century.

Margaret Bourke-White, one of the first staff photographers hired by *Life* magazine in 1936 and a world-renowned World War II photojournalist, always knew she was counted as a "gift" to her parents. From her earliest memories, she recalled her mother telling her, "Margaret, you can always be proud that you were invited into the world."

"I don't know where she got this fine philosophy that children should come because they were wanted and should not be the result of accidents," Margaret wrote in her autobiography titled *Portrait of Myself*. "When each of her own three children was on the way, Mother would say to those closest to her, 'I don't know whether this will be a boy or girl and I don't care. But this child was invited into the world and it will be a wonderful child.' She was explicit about the invitation and believed the child should be the welcomed result of a known and definite act of love between a man and woman."

Born to Joseph and Minnie White on June 14, 1904, in New York City, the middle child of three, Margaret Bourke-White grew up and went to school in Bound Brook, New Jersey. Her mother was a strong-willed Irish-Catholic, but Margaret would be an adult before she discovered that her father was born into an Orthodox Jewish family. When her parents married, they decided the children would be raised as Christian since her father was not particularly religious.

It was a progressive home for the time, advocating female equality and encouraging Margaret's ambitions to excel at whatever she did. Her mother set an example by taking up bicycling, although only men rode bicycles at the turn of the twentieth century. Even the use of slang was considered acceptable, and the children were allowed to chew gum, play cards, and read comic books. How scandalous!

> BEHOLD, CHILDREN ARE A GIFT OF THE LORD, THE FRUIT OF THE WOMB IS A REWARD.
>
> PSALM 127:3 NASB

But both of Margaret's parents set "high standards for their children," wrote Susan Goldman Rubin in *Margaret Bourke-White: Her Pictures Were Her Life*. Reading was encouraged, and Margaret and her siblings were taught the value of education and hard work.

The Whites drilled into their children that in life, "The only real handicap is fear," she wrote in her autobiography. "Be unafraid," they told her. "Go right up and look your fears in the face—and then do something." That philosophy of risk-taking prepared Margaret for the dangers she would later face as a photographer for *Life* magazine during World War II. It made her independent, self-confident, and fearless.

Margaret's father, an engineer-inventor, made his living as an industrial engineer in the printing business. He held several machine patents, including one for a Braille press for the blind. His excitement for modern technology and a love for photography rubbed off on Margaret, although she said it was not until after his death in 1922 that she began taking pictures. On vacations, he would be photographing bees and flowers, while Margaret was more interested in the subjects themselves, particularly snakes.

"I was very anxious to go to the jungle and do all the things women never did before," Margaret wrote in *Portrait of Myself*, "so I specialized in herpetology and studied reptiles hoping that sometime I would be good enough to be sent on an expedition."

Off she went to Columbia University at the age of seventeen, ready to conquer the biological world, but she was devastated when her father suffered a massive stroke and died while she was still in her freshman year. Due to financial problems, she switched universities several times, ending up at the University of Michigan at Ann Arbor majoring in zoology. A series of art photography classes made up her mind to switch to photography.

In 1924, she met and married Everett Chapman, an engineering student at the University of Michigan, and followed him to Purdue University, where he taught and she started taking classes. Chapman found a new job in Cleveland, and Margaret worked at the Natural History Museum there, while continuing her studies. The couple divorced two years later, and Margaret finally received a bachelor's degree in biology at Cornell University.

Unable to break into photography in New York City, she returned to Cleveland, where she found work in the new field of industrial photography, gaining a reputation for her photos of steel furnaces and assembly lines. Many of her photos appeared in the new magazine *Fortune*. With national recognition, she returned to New York City and worked part-time for Fortune, while freelancing for advertising agencies. In 1930, at the age of twenty-six, Margaret was earning more than $50,000 a year. She had become one of the most famous photojournalists in America.

In 1934, *Fortune* sent her to the Dust Bowl states during the Great Depression, where for four months she photographed the human drama of people whose land had dried up and literally blown away. It changed her outlook to meet these dispossessed people who had nothing left. For the rest of her life, people and their social problems became more important to Margaret than machines and products.

Following her success in photography there, she was sent to the Soviet Union to photograph some of the first images Americans had ever seen of that mysterious country, and in 1935 she photographed President Franklin D. Roosevelt and began documenting his public works projects. Margaret Bourke-White pioneered the photo essay for *Life* magazine in 1936 when its first issue hit the stands.

The next year, she teamed up with novelist Erskine Caldwell, whom she later married, on a book called *You Have Seen Their Faces*, about the tragedy of sharecroppers in the South. Critics called it her best work. She and Caldwell married in 1939, but divorced three years later, remaining childless. After two failed marriages, Margaret Bourke-White would never marry again.

Instead, when war knocked on the doors of America, Margaret was poised to document its evil. She was the first woman photographer ever attached to U. S. armed forces in World War II and the only Western photojournalist present when Germany invaded the Soviet Union. In 1942, while sailing on a troop ship headed for North Africa, the boat was torpedoed, killing hundreds. While abandoning ship with the survivors, she grabbed her Rolleiflex camera, and her photos were published later in a February 1943 edition of *Life* magazine.

By this time, Margaret's fearless courage was legendary. She accompanied U.S. troops when they invaded Italy, and she flew in the lead bomber of an Allied mission sent to wipe out a German-occupied airfield in Tunisia—while being shot at by German fighter planes.

At the end of the war, when General George Patton liberated Buchenwald—an infamous Nazi concentration camp—her photos remind us even today of the emaciated prisoners of war they found there. Later, at the Erla work camp, she photographed more than three hundred prisoners, who had been incinerated by Hitler's SS just hours before American troops arrived. Immediately after the war, Margaret Bourke-White's photos of a once beautiful Europe now in ruins were published in *Life*.

There were more stories to tell, and she would travel all over the world to tell them—to some thirty-six countries in all. In 1949 she published a book called *Halfway to Freedom*, with photos of Mohandas K. Gandhi at his spinning wheel, and in 1952, spent her last major assignment shooting a photo essay, depicting the effect of the Korean War on one family.

After she was diagnosed with Parkinson's disease sometime in the 1950s, Margaret could no longer hold a camera steady or traipse around the world in her signature leather jacket. Instead, for the last twenty years of her life, she was mostly confined to her house in Darien, Connecticut, fighting the debilitating disease.

Because Minnie White welcomed her into the world and instilled in her an independent spirit, Margaret Bourke-White became a pioneer for both women and her profession of photography, gaining the respect of the world for her unsurpassed record of its history.

A Mother of Influence lets her children know they were welcomed into the world.

LEONORA WHITAKER WOOD

Unknown

CATHERINE MARSHALL. Leonora's life as a mission teacher
in the hills of West Virginia inspired her daughter Catherine
Marshall to write the best-selling book Christy, which is
still touching the hearts of new generations of readers.

⋄⟨⟩⋄

Catherine Marshall followed her mother, Leonora, through the
rooms of the now abandoned mission house in Morgan Branch,
Tennessee, where the older woman had served as a nineteen-year-
old teacher in the early twentieth century. As they strolled through the
house, Leonora shared with her daughter the memories she had of each
room. It was not the first time Catherine had heard her mother's colorful
Appalachian stories. Catherine had been born in these hills and was
raised on the tales of the mountain people who lived here. It was, however, the first time she had ever seen the place for herself.

Leonora turned to her daughter and said, "This story aches to be told,
Catherine. The secrets of the human spirit . . . the wisdom . . . is needed
by so many today." Catherine knew it was true and that she needed to
share her mother's rich story with the world.

It began in the early 1900s when Leonora Whitaker attended a program at her church in Asheville, North Carolina, where a doctor had been
asked to speak. He wove a story about the journey he had made to
Morgan Branch, sharing with the congregation the plight of the intelligent yet dirt-poor mountain people he had met there. Because of his com-

passion for those people, he had founded a mission and told how desperately they needed missionaries to be a part of his work. As he spoke with such fervor, Leonora felt a stirring in her heart, drawing her to enlist as a volunteer — God calling her to leave home and family to be a teacher there.

> **DON'T YOU SEE THAT CHILDREN ARE GOD'S BEST GIFT? THE FRUIT OF THE WOMB HIS GENEROUS LEGACY?**
>
> PSALM 127:3 MSG

Some time later as she traveled to the mission, the rocking of the train lulled her into reverie, recalling the poignant farewells of her friends and family. As the train jolted to a stop at the tiny depot of Del Rio, she sat up, pulled her few things together, and stepped off the train into another world. As the train pulled away from the snow-covered station, leaving her completely alone, Leonora felt a stab of panic. Why was there no one to meet her? Didn't the doctor let the mission know she was coming?

Finally, Leonora spied a man carrying a pack and hurried to catch up to him. When she told him of her dilemma, he said that he was the mailman on his way to the mission. Despite his misgivings, she talked him into letting her go along with him. What she didn't know was that they were seven miles away from the mission and that she would be walking every step of the way through heavy snow, carrying her own baggage.

Eventually, the young Miss Whitaker reached the mission and began her life as a teacher. The mountain children, who came down from the wooded hills to the mission school, may have been poor and dressed in ragged clothes, but they were smart and willing to learn. At first Leonora thought she was the knowledgeable one, but she quickly found out she had a lot to learn as well.

Through women such as Flora Corn and her daughter, Opal, Leonora learned first-hand about the "clannish ways, their difficult lives, their fervent and varied superstitions, and their simple wisdom." She also found fierce friendship and patient teachers in most of the hill people, although a few of the more eccentric natives had to be won slowly. Many of the women were master quilters, and over time, as she lived in their midst, Leonora heard their legends sung in melodic ballads by men and women, young and old alike. She fell in love with her hill people and never forgot them. Some would become lifelong friends.

Later, Leonora met and married Presbyterian pastor John Wood, and they moved to Johnson City, Tennessee, where Sarah Catherine Wood (who would grow up to become the famous author Catherine Marshall) was born on September 27, 1914. Catherine attended high school in Keyser, West Virginia, where she was known as a normal busy teenager who played piano, was on the debate team, and was involved in scouting and church activities alike. As Leonora shared snippets of her life lived in Morgan Branch, a desire burned in Catherine's heart to write and teach, just as her mother had.

To fulfill her dream, Catherine enrolled in Agnes Scott College in Decatur, Georgia, where she majored in history. While attending Westminster Church in Atlanta, she first laid eyes on Pastor Peter Marshall, a dynamic Scottish preacher, who spoke to a standing-room-only crowd every Sunday. Eventually they met, fell in love, and were married. Peter was an amazing man whose sermons touched the hearts of those who were fortunate enough to hear him.

Soon he was asked to pastor New York Avenue Presbyterian, a prestigious church in Washington, D.C., where their only son, Peter, was born soon after. Catherine put aside her dream of becoming a writer and plunged into the role of mother and "good pastor's wife."

Life took several harsh turns for Catherine when in 1943 she contracted tuberculosis and spent two years in bed. Shortly after her recovery in 1946, her husband Peter suffered a frightening heart attack, but went on to serve two years as chaplain of the U.S. Senate. In 1949 Catherine's beloved Peter suffered a second heart attack, this one fatal. How would she—now a thirty-five-year-old single parent—survive?

God would comfort Catherine in a familiar way; she began to write again. At first, a publisher approached Catherine about editing a collection of Peter's sermons and prayers, which were issued in 1949 under the title *Mr. Jones, Meet the Master*. The book hit the best-seller list, and soon Catherine returned to her calling as a writer. Her 1951 biography about Peter Marshall, *A Man Called Peter*, was later made into a popular movie.

Years later Catherine agreed to visit Morgan Branch with her mother, Leonora, excited to put faces and landscape with all the names and places her mother had told her about. As she listened to her mother recalling the events of her days as a mission school-teacher, Catherine was able to imagine the people her mother talked about as they walked through the old mission house, rickety cabins, and along back roads filled with mud holes. When her questions were answered, Catherine sat down to write.

The book *Christy*, based on her mother's experiences as a young woman, was finished in 1967. Catherine had not only written about the people and events that took place in her mother's life but also about her mother's "genuine love and willing self-sacrifice for people she came to serve."

The impact of Leonora's life was far-reaching. Opal and her brother, Burl, whom Leonora had taught and inspired, attended Berea College. Burl became a civil engineer and assisted with the construction of the Golden Gate Bridge. Opal became a schoolteacher and purchased the property on which the mission stood when it closed down. Opal's son, Larry Myers, now greets visitors who come from around the world and tells them the stories of the people of Morgan Gap.

And *Christy*, inspired by the stories Leonora shared with her daughter, Catherine Marshall, is still touching and influencing a whole new generation of readers around the world.

A Mother of Influence leaves a legacy for the next generation.

MARGARET EVERTS MEARS

Unknown

HENRIETTA MEARS S mother Margaret

used every opportunity to instruct her daughter in spiritual

matters, assuring her later success as a Sunday school teacher

and writer and publisher of church curriculum.

⟨∞⟩

Three men—each forever impacted the world for Christ. The first, Billy Graham, became a well-known minister and author who has led hundreds of thousands of people to make a decision to follow Christ. The second, Bill Bright, founded Campus Crusade for Christ, which has shared the Gospel with university students in 180 countries. Richard Halverson, the third, became the U.S. Senate chaplain, whose duties included opening the Senate each day with prayer and also the counseling and spiritual care of senators and their families.

In addition to their soul-winning efforts, these three men had something more in common. Each was taught by an energetic Sunday school teacher named Henrietta Mears. This gifted teacher often wore flamboyant dresses and outrageous hats and had a passion for teaching young people about the Bible.

Henrietta Mears came from a rich spiritual heritage over flowing in a long line of ministers, which included her grandfather, Dr. W. W. Everts—a prominent pastor. Her grandmother's life closely resembled Henrietta's in belief and practice. While reading the biography of Margaret Burtis Everts, Henrietta said, "I'm amazed to see how many of my own policies and beliefs trace back to my grandmother. The same thinking, the same ideas and approach. She taught them to my mother, and I was almost unconsciously reared on these same precepts." It is no surprise then that her own mother shared many of Henrietta's qualities.

Henrietta's mother, Margaret Everts, was born into the household of these two amazing Christian examples. She grew into a highly intelligent woman with a deep relationship with Christ and married E. Ashley Mears, a wealthy bank owner known for his "optimism, humor, clear sense of vision, and an extraordinary capacity to train people."

> [JESUS SAID,] "AS FOR WHAT WAS SOWN ON GOOD SOIL, THIS IS THE ONE WHO HEARS THE WORD AND UNDERSTANDS IT, WHO INDEED BEARS FRUIT AND YIELDS, IN ONE CASE A HUN- DREDFOLD, IN ANOTHER SIXTY, AND IN ANOTHER THIRTY."
>
> MATTHEW 13:23 NRSV

Margaret was a caring mother—full of enthusiasm and concern for her family and others—who reached out to the poor with great acts of charity. And as a natural evangelist, Margaret would share the Gospel with any salesman who happened to knock at her door. The gift of hospitality was a strong part of her evangelistic streak, which allowed her family to bond easily with friends and strangers alike so they could share their close and personal relationship with Christ.

Margaret gave birth to her seventh child, Henrietta Cornelia Mears, in Fargo, North Dakota, on October 23, 1890. Henrietta accepted Christ when she was only seven years old and began her lifelong calling as a Sunday school teacher only five years later at the age of twelve.

Even as a child, Henrietta and her mother spent hours gardening together. Henrietta loved the vibrant colors and sweet smells of the flowers and the finished product of vegetables and fruits they tended. North Dakota summers were short, and it was wonderful to work alongside her mother, who never let an opportunity pass to teach her precocious daughter about Christ.

One summer Henrietta, eager for her radishes to fully mature, pulled them out of the ground to check their progress and then tried to replant them. Her mother used Henrietta's impatience as an opportunity to teach her daughter about spiritual growth—that it should not be rushed, but rather fed and watered, basking in the light of Christ and allowed to grow naturally.

Henrietta decided quite early in life that God wanted her to teach, but her dreams were challenged when Henrietta's doctor told her that an eye condition would blind her before the age of thirty. She was so convinced that God was guiding her life that she studied all the harder in school. After graduating from the University of Minnesota with honors, Henrietta taught high school chemistry. Although she was always extremely nearsighted, she never did completely lose her sight.

In 1928 Henrietta Mears accepted the position of director of Christian education at the First Presbyterian Church of Hollywood where, as she labored faithfully, two things happened. She completely overhauled the Sunday school materials used at the church, and Sunday school attendance jumped from four hundred and fifty to four thousand. As she went through the curriculum, she had found it to be outdated and not even biblically based, so she returned it to the publisher and wrote her own. Her material, which was said to be "bold, challenging, and captivating," made Scripture come alive.

News about her curriculum soon spread all across the country, and she began receiving requests from other churches to send them copies. The demand for her material was so great that in 1933, Miss Mears helped found a publishing company, which still publishes Sunday school curriculum today under the name Gospel Light Publishing.

During her tenure at Hollywood's First Presbyterian Church, Miss Mears influenced a number of Hollywood stars, who were welcomed into her home. She also started a retreat center called Forest Home where people could get away to spend time with God, including thousands of children and teens who found Christ at her camps.

On March 20, 1963, Henrietta Mears left this earth for Heaven. She is remembered for so many godly traits, among them a boundless energy, enthusiasm for life, single-minded devotion to God, and a real passion for the Word of God. She was loved for her infectious laughter, crazy hats, and wise words. As her mother had handed down a rich heritage of spiritual lessons to Henrietta, she in turn passed them on to the world.

A Mother of Influence uses the ordinary things of life to teach her children about Christ.

MABEL SUFFIELD TOLKIEN

1870 - 1904

J. R. R. TOLKIEN. Mabel's devotion to her son J.R.R. Tolkien

enabled him to create the fantastic Middle-Earth stories

that would captivate the hearts and minds of millions.

⚬⚭⚬

From the deck of the steamer *Roslin Castle*, a young woman named Mabel Suffield waved good-bye to her family and friends, knowing she would not see them again for many years. After a three-year engagement to Arthur Tolkien, her family had finally consented to the marriage. She was now leaving England for South Africa where Arthur had accepted a post at the Bank of Africa.

Mabel found life in South Africa quite different from that in England. Wolves and jackals roamed the open prairies a few hundred yards from their house, monkeys occasionally caused havoc in their yard, and venomous snakes could be found hiding in the woodshed. Summers were extremely hot, winters were cold and dry, and year-round dust from the dirt streets filled the air.

"Owlin' Wilderness! Horrid Waste!" is how she described her situation in a letter to her family back home.

The couple's first child, John Ronald Reuel Tolkien, was born on January 3, 1892. A sickly child by nature, young Ronald did not fare well in the harsh South African climate, and he spent much of his early years in bed with one illness or another. When his brother Hillary was born in 1894, Mabel decided it was time to take the young boys back to England for a while so that Ronald could recuperate in the cooler air.

Arthur, busy with his duties at the bank, was unable to join them on their journey but promised he would meet them in England a short time later. It was a promise he was unable to keep. Several months later, Mabel received word that Arthur had contracted rheumatic fever. When his condition failed to improve, she made arrangements to return to South Africa, but it was too late. A few days later, a telegram arrived informing her that Arthur had died.

Mabel now began the difficult process of raising and shaping the lives of her two young boys on her own. With little means of support, she decided to move out of her family's home to the English countryside just outside of Birmingham, where the boys would be free to explore their surroundings and not feel the strain of the poverty that hung over their lives.

To a young boy with a vivid and growing imagination such as Ronald's, life in the country was a magical place filled with exciting adventures and interesting characters. It was also a place where Ronald would first encounter people with a different dialect from his own. They used such words as "miskin" for dustbin and "gamgee" for cotton wool.

"Any corner of that country," Tolkien would later remark, "however fair or squalid, is in an indefinable way 'home' to me, as no other part of the world is."

Of course, it was not all fun and games for the boys, for Mabel wanted them to have the best education so they could one day attend the prestigious King Edward's School in Birmingham. Taking it upon herself to educate her sons, she soon discovered that Ronald had a special affinity for languages. She introduced him to Latin (which he liked very much) and French (which he liked much less). Mabel also encouraged Ronald's love of drawing during these years, instructing him in botany as he eagerly sketched the plants and trees that grew around his home.

When class was not in session, Mabel was careful to provide the boys with a variety of storybooks for them to enjoy. Ronald found mythical tales of brave young knights slaying fearsome dragons to be the most compelling, especially the tale of Sigurd slaying the dragon Fafnir (a story in the *Red Fairy Book* by Andrew Lang).

"I desired dragons with a profound desire," he later stated. "Of course I, in my timid body did not wish to have them in the neighborhood. But the world that contained even the imagination of Fafnir was richer and more beautiful, at whatever cost or peril."

At the age of seven, Tolkien began to compose his own tales of dragons, which he delighted in reading to his patient mother. Of course, being the perennial teacher, Mabel couldn't help but correct her young boy on his misuse of English grammar, even at his young age.

"My mother said nothing about the dragon," Tolkien later recalled, "but pointed out that one could not say 'a green great dragon,' but had to say 'a great green dragon.' I wondered why, and still do."

Sadly, in April of 1904, when Tolkien was just twelve years old, his mother was diagnosed with diabetes. Insulin treatment was not yet available in those days, and though she rallied during the summer months, her condition again deteriorated in the fall. Near the beginning of November she collapsed suddenly at her home, sank into a diabetic coma, and died shortly thereafter.

> MY HEART OVERFLOWS WITH A GOOD THEME; I ADDRESS MY VERSES TO THE KING; MY TONGUE IS THE PEN OF A READY WRITER.
>
> PSALM 45:1 NASB

Though she was in his life only a short time, Mabel's guidance enabled Tolkien to delve into his creativity and develop the love of language that would play such an integral role in novels such as *The Hobbit* and *The Lord of the Rings*.

But the greatest contribution she would make to Tolkien's life was to instill in him her indefatigable faith in Christ. Marching her sons to St. Anne's church near the center of Birmingham each Sunday, Mabel made sure that both Ronald and Hillary had gained a firm foundation in Christ by the time of her death.

It was a faith that Tolkien would carry with him for the rest of his life, not only through his darkest days, fighting in the trenches of World War I, but also through his happiest days, serving as Merton Professor of English Language and Literature at Oxford University. It was also a faith that would shape his view of the world and influence all of the stories he wrote that would later challenge and inspire others.

"*The Lord of the Rings* is of course a fundamentally religious and Catholic work," Tolkien would write in a 1953 letter to a Jesuit friend. "Unconsciously so at first, but consciously in the revision. That is why I have not put in, or have cut out, practically all references to anything like 'religion,' to cults or practices, in the imaginary world. For the religious element is absorbed into the story and the symbolism."

Although Tolkien's mother died while he was still a young boy, her faith in Christ and her desire to shape his education through the proper use of language was a major influence on his life's work.

A Mother of Influence teaches her children that language is an important tool.

MARY FRANCES PAXTON PENNEY

1842-1913

J. C. PENNEY. Because of Mary Frances Penney's faith and the family's adherence to the Golden Rule, J.C. Penney founded a retail empire based on integrity and loyalty.

⟨∞⟩

When James Cash (J.C.) Penney was only eight years old, his father, the Reverend J.C. Penney, Sr., told his son that he would have to start buying his own clothes. An unpaid preacher for the Primitive Baptists, his father wanted to teach his son self-reliance and the value of a dollar. That year the young entrepreneur earned enough to buy a pair of shoes.

Born September 16, 1875, on the family farm near Hamilton, Missouri, J.C. Penney was the seventh of twelve children, only six of whom made it to adulthood. His father farmed to make a living, and his mother, Mary, a genteel southern woman from Kentucky and a devout woman of faith, worked hard alongside him as a farmer's wife.

According to the J.C. Penney Company History Brochure, his mother's main contribution to her son's upbringing was teaching him "the value of service to others by example in the way she lived her life for the benefit of those around her."

One of J.C.'s enterprises to earn money was raising pigs. He bought one, fattened it up, and sold it for a profit. With the profits, he bought more pigs, as well as piglets, and repeated the process. When the neighbors objected to the hog stench, J.C.'s father made him sell the pigs, and he turned instead to raising and selling watermelons.

There was no money to attend college, so after graduating from

Hamilton High School in 1893, J.C. Penney worked on the family farm until he secured work in 1895 as a clerk in a local dry-goods and clothing store. The job paid twenty-five dollars a month. The work was hard on the young man, who had never been particularly athletic or hearty physically, and in less than two years, his doctor recommended he relocate to Colorado to recover his health. There, he worked for a couple of stores before buying a butcher shop, but quickly went bankrupt when he refused to bribe the cook of a local hotel with whiskey to get their business. Penney always took the moral high road.

> **JESUS SAID, "DO FOR OTHERS WHAT YOU WOULD LIKE THEM TO DO FOR YOU. THIS IS A SUMMARY OF ALL THAT IS TAUGHT IN THE LAW AND THE PROPHETS."**
>
> MATTHEW 7:12 NLT

Later he would open up a new Golden Rule Store in the town of Kemmerer, Wyoming, with one-third of the money coming from Penney. As part-owner, he now shared in the profits and dreamed of having a chain of his own someday, based on the Golden Rule principles. Always frugal because of his childhood poverty, Penney lived over the store in an attic room to conserve money.

In speaking of those years, J.C. Penney said, "In setting up a business under the name and meaning of the Golden Rule, I was publicly binding myself, in my business relations, to a principle which had been a real and intimate part of my family upbringing. To me the sign on the store was much more than a trade name. We took our slogan 'Golden Rule Store' with strict literalness. Our idea was to make money and build business through serving the community with fair dealing and honest value."

In 1907 J.C. Penney bought out his partners in the Golden Rule stores and in 1909 set up his headquarters in Salt Lake City, Utah. By January of 1913 he incorporated the chain of stores and changed the name to J.C. Penney Company. By 1914, Penney owned forty-eight stores and decided to move his headquarters to the seat of business in New York City. Growth continued at an exponential rate, with five hundred stores by 1924 and more than a thousand by 1927. By then he was chairman of the board, acting in that capacity until 1946.

Penney had some pretty strict rules for his employees: no alcohol or tobacco use. He didn't believe in it for himself, and he didn't think they should either. But he did believe in them as people with potential.

"Anyone and everyone has in him the latent capacity to become a human dynamo," he once said, "capable of accomplishing anything to which he aspires." Loyalty and integrity were the character traits he expected of his "associates," as he called his employees, just as he expected the same high standards of himself.

In his autobiography, *The Man with a Thousand Partners*, J.C. Penney wrote "the ethical means by which my business associates and I have made money is more important than the fact that we have achieved business success."

He was well advanced in years before he committed his life fully to Jesus Christ. A good, honest man, who attended church, in his early years he was primarily interested in becoming a success and making money. As a clerk working for six dollars a week at Joslin's Dry Goods Store in Denver, he had an ambition to one day be worth one hundred thousand dollars. When he reached that goal he felt temporary satisfaction, but soon set his sights on being worth a million dollars.

Both Mr. and Mrs. Penney worked hard to expand their business, but one day Mrs. Penney caught cold and developed pneumonia, which subsequently caused her death. "When she died," Penney recalled, "my world crashed about me. To build a business, to make a success in the eyes of men, to accumulate money—what was the purpose of life? I felt mocked by life, even by God himself."

Before long, Penney was ruined financially and in deep distress. It was at that point that he turned to God and experienced a true spiritual conversion. He said, "When I was brought to humility and the knowledge of dependence on God, sincerely and earnestly seeking God's aid, it was forthcoming, and a light illumined my being. I cannot otherwise describe it than to say that it changed me as a man."

In 1925, in memory of his parents, who had struggled and sacrificed to serve God, J.C. Penney built the Memorial Home Community for retired religious workers in Florida at a personal cost of $1.25 million.

The last days of Penney's life were spent in many charitable and religious activities, committed to organizations such as the Young Men's Christian Association, National 4-H Club, and the Boy Scouts, as well as many others. His mother's faith and adherence to the Golden Rule was a shining beacon, which guided Penney until his death at the age of ninety-five.

A Mother of Influence teaches
her children to live by the Golden Rule.

PAULA BONHOEFFER

Unknown

DIETRICH BONHOEFFER'S mother Paula, who encouraged idealism in her children, instilled in her Lutheran minister son the values that would help him resist the Nazis.

⌒∞⌒

One of the twentieth century's most widely known and admired martyrs, Lutheran theologian Dietrich Bonhoeffer, once wrote that like Christ, "the Christian must involve himself in the alleviation of hunger, injustice and all the other worldly miseries." His beliefs assured his death at the hands of the Nazis in the final days of World War II, shortly before Germany was liberated by the Allies.

Born on February 4, 1906, in Breslau, Prussia, a few short minutes before his twin sister, Sabine, Dietrich was the son of Karl and Paula Bonhoeffer. Karl was a renowned psychiatrist and a leading professor of neurology and psychiatry, and his mother, Paula, was the granddaughter of a famous church historian.

Bonhoeffer's childhood was idyllic, perhaps because his life would be cut short prematurely. He was the sixth of eight children, and the house bustled with activity, presided over by his mother. The children's laughter at one another's jokes, singing, and playing games were encouraged by Paula Bonhoeffer, always in the context of what it means to live a joyful Christian life. She expected her children to live virtuous lives and instilled her own idealism into their worldview.

The Bonhoeffer children and their parents lived in a huge comfortable house in Breslau, Germany, where they were cared for by a nanny and two servants. In the summer Dietrich and his siblings spent most of their daylight hours playing in the hills and forests of the Harz Mountains, where they would spend the warmer months in a house there.

At the age of six, Dietrich and his family moved to Berlin, Germany, where his father taught psychiatry and neurology at Berlin University. He started school at seven, and by ten, was reading the German classics. All who met him when he was a boy were impressed by his goodness, warm personality, and love of God.

During World War I, Dietrich's brother Walter was killed in battle, and he and his sister Sabine talked for hours at a time about the meaning of life and death. It was at the age of fourteen that Bonhoeffer began considering the ministry as his profession. Sabine wrote that Dietrich had "the gift of perfect assurance of manners; he listened attentively and attached a great value to dealing politely with other people and keeping a certain distance—not from haughtiness, but from respect of the other's personality on which he did not want to impinge."

After World War I, Germans suffered staggering rates of inflation, and even to buy a loaf of bread, the Bonhoeffers would have to carry a bag of money to the store. It was the beginning of the economic conditions that would foster Hitler's rise to power.

Bonhoeffer, a brilliant student, received his doctorate in theology from Berlin University in 1927. He was only twenty-one and would become a powerful voice in speaking out against Nazism. By the 1930s Hitler's Nazi regime was vigorously spreading its doctrine of supremacy of the Aryan (white) race, which included ridding the world of such "inferior" races as the Jews, along with gypsies and mentally or physically disabled people.

Dietrich Bonhoeffer made no secret of his hatred for Nazism and dedicated his life to ending Hitler's reign of terror. To oppose the Nazi-sponsored "German Christian" church, Bonhoeffer helped to found the Pastors' Emergency League, which became the Confessing Church of Germany. By 1935 he instituted an underground seminary in Finkenwalde to train pastors for their illegal church, which had been banned by the Nazis.

Because of continued Gestapo harassment, friends urged Bonhoeffer to leave the country, so he agreed to a speaking tour in America. However, after six weeks, when it was obvious war was inevitable, he returned to Germany in mid-summer of 1939.

By the next year, he was fully involved in the German resistance movement in an effort to overthrow Hitler and, if necessary, assassinate the dictator. He worked as a courier for the Counter-Espionage Service, using his church contacts around the world, and even risked his life in 1942 to smuggle seven Jews to Switzerland.

After an unsuccessful attempt on Hitler's life, Bonhoeffer was arrested on April 5, 1943, and taken to Tegel Prison because of his part in the plot. Speaking to another prisoner at the time about humanity's obligation to fight evil, Bonhoeffer said, "If a drunken driver is at the wheel, it is not just the minister's job to comfort the relations of those he has killed, but if possible to seize the steering wheel."

> WHEN THE LAMB BROKE THE FIFTH SEAL, I SAW UNDER THE ALTAR THE SOULS OF ALL WHO HAD BEEN MARTYRED FOR THE WORD OF GOD AND FOR BEING FAITHFUL IN THEIR WITNESS.
>
> REVELATION 6:9 NLT

Every prisoner who spent time with Bonhoeffer, as well as his jailers, spoke of the minister's compassion and concern for others. "Bonhoeffer . . . was all humility and sweetness," wrote Payne Best, an English officer imprisoned with him. "He always seemed to diffuse an atmosphere of happiness, of joy in every smallest event in life, and a deep gratitude for the mere fact that he was alive."

The last letter written to his mother five months before he was hanged, said, "Thank you for all the love that has come to me in my cell from you during the past year, it has made every day easier for me. My wish for you and Father and Maria [his fiancé] and for all of us is that the New Year may bring us at least an occasional glimmer of light and that we may once more have the joy of living together. May God keep you both well."

On July 27, 1945, while listening to BBC radio, Karl and Paula Bonhoeffer learned that their son Dietrich had been executed when Bishop Bell and other clergy in England broadcast his memorial service.

Because Dietrich Bonhoeffer's mother guided her son into a virtuous life, teaching him to love good and hate evil, his courage to stand up for the principles of faith still inspire today.

A Mother of Influence teaches her children to discern between good and evil.

MERCY CROSBY

Unknown

FANNY CROSBY. Mercy Crosby, whose daughter, Fanny Crosby,

would become one of the most prolific authors of gospel

hymn texts ever, was totally devoted to her only daughter.

⚜

"When I was six weeks old," Fanny Crosby once wrote about her tragic blindness, "a slight cold caused inflammation of the eyes. Our usual doctor was away from home, so a stranger was called in. He recommended the use of hot poultices, which practically destroyed my sight. When this sad calamity became known, the unfortunate man thought it best to leave the neighborhood, and we never heard of him again.

"But," she continued, "I have not, for a moment, in more than eighty-five years, felt a spark of resentment against him; for I have always believed that the good Lord, in His infinite mercy, by this means consecrated me to the work that I am still permitted to do. When I remember how I have been blessed, how can I repine?"

Frances "Fanny" Jane Crosby, was born on March 24, 1820, in the tiny village of Southeast in Putnam County, New York, to farmers John and Mercy Crosby. Fanny never knew her father, who died in the same year she was born. Her mother, who lived to be more than ninety-one years old, became a maid.

Shortly after, Fanny and her mother, Mercy, moved to North Salem, New York, and in 1928, on to Ridgefield, Connecticut, where Fanny lived with her grandmother, who was a great influence on her life.

"She was a woman of exemplary piety, and a firm believer in prayer," Fanny wrote. "At eventime she often used to call me to her dear old rocking-chair, where we would kneel and pray together." When Fanny came up against an obstacle, prayer was her first point of action.

Despite her near blindness, Fanny passionately longed for education. One night when she was eleven years old, she prayed that a door would open for her to learn.

"It was twilight," she wrote, "and grandmother and I both sat talking in the old rocking-chair. Then we knelt and prayed together, after which she went away. I crept toward the window, and through the branches of a giant oak that stood outside, the soft moonlight fell upon my head like the benediction of an angel. I knelt, and repeated over and over again these simple words, 'Dear Lord, please show me how I can learn like other children.' At that moment the anxiety that had burdened my heart was changed to the sweet consciousness that my prayer would be answered in due time.

"Four years later," she wrote, "I had been out, and on my return mother met me at the gate. I heard a paper rustling in her hand. It was a circular, my mother told me, from the New York Institution for the Blind, sent her by a friend." Fanny was delighted. God had answered her prayer just as she knew He would.

Fanny knew that she could learn. For a while, they had lived with a Mrs. Hawley, a kind Christian woman who recognized Fanny's intelligence and set her to memorizing Scripture. After two years, Fanny had memorized the entire Pentateuch — even the dry genealogies — most of the poetic books, and the four Gospels.

When she was fourteen, four months after her mother brought home the advertisement, Fanny made the trip to New York to begin her adventure in learning. She said that leaving her mother caused her great distress, but she was determined to make any sacrifice necessary to get an education.

At the New York Institute for the Blind, she mastered almost every course (she hated math), but loved grammar so much that she memorized the entire text of Brown's Grammar! She became a teacher and well-known for her poetry published in New York newspapers, the *Saturday Evening Post*, and four books of poetry.

While attending a Methodist meeting in 1850, the Calvinist Miss

> **WHAT A STACK OF BLESSING YOU HAVE PILED UP FOR THOSE WHO WORSHIP YOU, READY AND WAITING FOR ALL WHO RUN TO YOU TO ESCAPE AN UNKIND WORLD.**
>
> PSALM 31:19 MSG

Crosby, experienced a profound "born again" experience, and over the next forty years, she wrote at least nine thousand hymn texts, many of them for Sunday school songs. She was so prolific that her publishers used more than two hundred pen names for her to disguise the fact they were using so much of her material!

Because of her mother and grandmother's devotion to her as a child, Fanny Crosby's hymns have been sung in every church and carried around the world by thousands of missionaries, blessing millions of people.

A Mother of Influence devotes herself to her children's needs.

LILLA CHARLTON HESTON

Unknown

CHARLTON HESTON'S mother, Lilla, a woman of indomitable

courage, taught her movie star son to face life head-on.

❦

Charlton Heston felt he had so much to be thankful for as he stood with his wife Lydia, surrounded by family and friends at the Nikko Hotel, celebrating their fiftieth wedding anniversary. Both of his children, Fraser and Holly, brought tears to his eyes as they spoke lovingly of their parents. Then there was their amazing grandson Jack, whom they adored.

Famous singer Mel Torme even dropped by to croon "Our Love Is Here to Stay," though he was leaving that night for a concert in Australia. But one important person was missing from the noisy room filled with well-known actors, military generals, government officials, and friends the couple had made throughout the years. Charlton Heston's mother, Lilla — the woman who had been such an influence on her son's life for so many years — was too sick and frail to travel.

Born in Chicago, Illinois, near the turn of the twentieth century, Lilla Charlton was raised by her grandparents after her father and mother divorced. With her mother and sister, Lilla moved into the household of her grandfather, James Charlton, and two unmarried aunts. Her grandfather was the solitary male in the all-female group and was said to have been "the strongest male influence" in Lilla's life. To give the girls a name and a family to belong to, Charlton adopted Lilla and her sister, making him not only their grandfather, but their father as well. His decision culd-

BE STRONG AND
LET YOUR HEART
TAKE COURAGE, ALL
YOU WHO HOPE IN
THE **LORD.**

PSALM 31:24 NASB

pulted Lilla and her sister into a new world of fine schools and trips to Europe as they grew into womanhood.

Soon after meeting Russell Whitford Carter, a handsome and charming man with a deep voice, Lilla and he were married and bought a small house on Lake Michigan near Chicago. Here on October 4, 1923, John Charlton Carter (Charlton Heston) was born. His parents divorced within a few years, and sometime later Lilla married Chester Heston, who gave Charlton his name and moved the family into Chicago.

Charlton Heston has said he doesn't ever remember a time when he didn't want to be an actor. Heston's first big role in the Academy Award-winning picture *The Greatest Show on Earth* made him a star, and he went on to play the leads in such epic films as *The Ten Commandments* and *The Greatest Story Ever Told*. He won the Academy Award for best actor for his role in Ben Hur. He once wrote that his mother Lilla was always there for him, saying of her that she was a woman of "indomitable courage"—a kind of heroine like Jane Eyre. She lived through a century of change yet always faced life bravely.

While filming a movie in Utah, Charlton Heston received the call he had always dreaded. His mother had died in the night at age ninety-six. He would miss her terribly but later wrote that he knew "she'd had a long, rich life, full of travel, adventure, children and grandchildren— people she loved. She lived to hold her great-grandson in her lap." Because of her courage to face life head-on, whether times were good or bad, Lilla felt she had lived the "good life," and so did her son.

A Mother of Influence teaches her children to face life with courage.

SARAH (SALLY) STONE BARTON

Unknown

CLARA BARTON. Sarah Barton passed on her strong will

and practical common sense to her daughter, Clara,

founder of the American Red Cross.

༒

S ally Barton worried so much about her daughter Clara's many fears that she consulted a phrenologist, who told her to, "Throw responsibility upon her. As soon as age will permit, give her a school to teach." Sally Barton heeded his counsel, and at the age of fifteen, Clara began an eighteen-year teaching career.

Born Clarissa Harlowe Barton on Christmas Day, 1821, in North Oxford, Massachusetts, to Stephen and Sarah Barton, the large family nicknamed her "Clara." Ten years younger than her four siblings, Clara was an emotionally shy and supersensitive young girl.

Stephen Barton, a typical, hard-working New England farmer and intelligent local politician, was devoted to his wife and five children, although he and his younger wife, Sally, didn't always get along. The couple had married when she was only seventeen, and he was thirty; she was strong-willed and hot-tempered, and he was "calm, sound, reasonable."

Clara's two older brothers and two older sisters doted on her, and some would have said she was spoiled. She learned how to ride bareback, pound nails, and tie knots from her brothers, while her mother and sisters taught her the more feminine arts of cooking, sewing, making soap, and gardening. Her father, who had fought in the Indian wars, told Clara tales about his army experiences, and when her brother David was injured during a barn-raising, she learned nursing techniques to take care of his

GOD HATH NOT
GIVEN US THE SPIRIT
OF FEAR; BUT OF
POWER, AND OF
LOVE, AND OF A
SOUND MIND.

2 TIMOTHY 1:7 KJV

needs until his recovery two years later. All of those skills would prove useful in the future when she braved the Civil War battlefields to tend the wounded.

In 1850 Sally Barton died, long before her daughter achieved a worldwide reputation. Because Clara had been working in Washington, D.C. for more than a decade in the Patent Office when the Civil War broke out, she leaped into the cause of the Union. After she heard stories of great suffering due to lack of supplies at the Battle of Bull Run, Clara ran an ad in the *Worcester Spy*, asking for provisions to help the wounded. With the enormous outpouring of help, she set up an organization to distribute what was given, which would be the forerunner of the American Red Cross.

In July 1862 she persuaded Surgeon-General Hammond to allow her "to go upon the sick transports in any direction, for the purpose of distributing comforts for the sick and wounded, and nursing them."

On the battlefield, with skirt pinned up to her waist, Clara extracted bullets from bleeding wounds, held the hands of dying soldiers, and served them whatever food was available, usually gruel. When she ran out of field dressings, she substituted corn stalks, something her mother would have found to be quite practical and a good use of Clara's common sense. Once when she was crossing a river to tend soldiers at Fredericksburg, however, she nearly lost her life. She wrote later that she could barely walk because of her blood-soaked skirts.

"In my feeble estimation," wrote the chief surgeon, "General McClellan, with all his laurels, sinks into insignificance beside the true heroine of the age, the angel of the battlefield." The name stuck, and Clara Barton would always be known for her qualities of mercy and courage. The American Red Cross is a testament to Clara Barton's perseverance and fortitude in helping people during times of disaster and war.

Even though Clara Barton was shy and fearful as a child, Sally Barton passed on her practical common sense, as well as her strong will, without which her daughter could not have achieved so much.

A Mother of Influence helps her children overcome their fears.

ADA MAE WILKEY DAY

Unknown

SUPREME COURT JUSTICE SANDRA DAY O'CONNOR'S

mother, Ada Mae, insisted on a quality education for

her daughter, despite living on a remote Arizona ranch.

∞

The Lazy B Ranch—all 155,000 acres of it—lies in the high desert plateau on the Arizona-New Mexico border, south of the Gila River. Established in the 1880s by Sandra Day O'Connor's grandfather, Henry Clay Day, when Arizona was still a territory, most of the land is covered with scrub brush. Kit Carson called this part of the world "god-forsaken" because there was so little rainfall.

To deliver their first child, Harry and Ada Mae Day traveled more than two hundred miles to El Paso, Texas, for the birth. Then Ada Mae brought her baby girl Sandra home to a four-room adobe house, with no running water and no electricity. The nearest town was thirty miles away, so there was no school within driving distance. Prospects for the little girl's future seemed nonexistent, but Harry and Ada Mae were determined to "stitch learning" into their children.

Ada Mae, who had a college education, subscribed to metropolitan newspapers and magazines and read *The Wall Street Journal*, *The New Yorker*, and the *Saturday Evening Post* to her daughter hour after hour. When Sandra was four years old, Ada Mae began using the Calvert method of homeschooling, but later sent her daughter to live with Sandra's grandmother in El Paso, where she attended a private girls' school.

One summer Ada Mae and Harry took their children on an educational car trip to visit all the state capitols west of the Mississippi River.

[THE LORD SAID,]
"SEE, I HAVE
REFINED YOU, BUT
NOT LIKE SILVER; I
HAVE TESTED YOU IN
THE FURNACE
OF ADVERSITY."

ISAIAH 48:10 NRSV

Usually though, the summer months were spent working on the ranch, where Sandra's friends were her parents, sister Ann, brother Alan, the ranch hands, some wild hogs, and Bob the bobcat.

Young Sandra skipped two grades, graduating from high school at age sixteen, and then attended Stanford University. With a major in economics, the bright young woman earned a B.A. degree with honors in 1950 and went on to law school there, where she edited the Stanford Law Review.

Eventually, Sandra married John Jay O'Connor, also a law student, and in her early career she served as a deputy district attorney. But when her three sons came along, Sandra Day O'Connor only worked part-time in a law office, did volunteer work, and was active in civic affairs so that she could put marriage and children first. Known as a hard worker, O'Connor also was politically active in the Republican Party.

When she resumed a full-time career, O'Connor served in Arizona state government until appointment by the governor to a partial term as an Arizona state senator and then was elected twice to that seat. Later, after serving as a Superior Court judge, O'Connor was chosen to sit on the Arizona Court of Appeals, and in 1981 appointed by President Ronald Reagan as the first woman justice to the Supreme Court of the United States.

Justice Sandra Day O'Connor's mother, Ada Mae, never let the circumstances of their hard western lifestyle prevent the education of her oldest daughter. O'Connor has served on the Supreme Court with distinction, proving that in America, it doesn't matter how you begin in life; it's where you end up that counts.

A Mother of Influence lets the difficulties of life teach her children to overcome adversity.

SUE WARNER

Unknown

KURT WARNER. With love and strength, Kurt Warner's mother,

Sue, taught her Super Bowl-winning son to always trust God.

⌐◯◯◯⌐

Kurt Warner stood on the sidelines, watching as Al Del Greco of the Tennessee Titans successfully kicked a forty-three-yard field goal with two minutes left in the Super Bowl, capping a sixteen-point run by the Titans that tied the game. Around him, coaches and players paced nervously, wondering if their incredible season was about to come to an unhappy end.

However, as Kurt Warner stepped onto the field, he couldn't stop smiling. "It was a daunting situation," he recalls in his autobiography, *All Things Possible*, "but I wasn't worried about the possibility of pulling the biggest choke job in Super Bowl history. Blowing a sixteen-point lead at the Super Bowl is nothing to get freaked out about." Stepping back onto the field, Warner would put together a drive that included a seventy-three-yard touchdown pass to win the game.

From a young age, Warner had learned to have confidence in his abilities and put his trust in God. After his parents divorced, Kurt and his brother were raised by their mother, Sue Warner, who modeled strength and motivation for them during those formative years.

"One lesson my mom helped instill in me is that it's no use moping about your circumstances," he noted in *All Things Possible*. "The worst thing you can do is concern yourself with things that are out of your control."

Sue Warner encouraged her boys to get involved in activities at school, such as sports and music, but was careful not to let them get too competitive. When Kurt began to gain recognition for his accomplish-

[JESUS SAID,] "WITH GOD ALL THINGS ARE POSSIBLE."

MARK 10:27 KJV

ments on the football field, she made certain that his brother always knew he was just as important. "She fostered an atmosphere of togetherness," noted Kurt.

Above all, Sue Warner was active in her children's spiritual lives, taking them to church every Sunday. "I credit my mom for being so adamant about keeping God in our lives and instilling the discipline that kept me on the right path," he wrote in his autobiography. It was this foundation that would enable him to trust in God after being cut from the Green Bay Packers in 1994 and persevere in the Arena Football League and NFL Europe until he won a starting quarterback position for the St. Louis Rams.

In the conclusion to *All Things Possible*, Kurt expressed his appreciation to his mother for the influence she had on his life: "Mom, thank you for your love, strength and sacrifices over the years . . . your support has been second to none, and I thank you for the values you instilled in me."

Kurt Warner's life as a star football player is a testament to his mother's love, support, and unwavering faith in God.

A Mother of Influence teaches her children to trust in God.

JOHANNA HENRIKE CHRISTIANE NISSEN BRAHMS

1789-1865

JOHANNES BRAHMS' mother, Christiane, encouraged her son to not only be a good musician, but a good person as well, developing in him a benevolent nature that would endear him to the world.

✦

Johannes Brahms, one of the greatest musicians who ever lived, wrote his masterpieces in almost every classical form of music except opera. His greatest works include *The German Requiem*, performed year after year at Christmastime in countries around the world, and *Lullaby and Good Night*, possibly the most famous lullaby ever written.

Johannes Brahms was born in 1833 in Hamburg, Germany, where his father, Johann Jakob Brahms, played double bass in the city's bars and slums. From him, Johannes inherited health, ambition, and an incredible musical talent that would enable him to become one of the most famous composers in history.

At the time of his birth, his mother, Christiane—a frail, unattractive woman of forty-four-walked with a bit of a limp because one of her legs was shorter than the other. But it never affected her ability as a mother. A tender and dedicated parent, with a remarkable intellect, Christiane might have had even more impact on Johannes' compositions than his father because of the love and nurture she lavished on her serious young son. From her, Johannes inherited a sensible and kindhearted disposition that

A GENEROUS MAN
WILL PROSPER; HE
WHO REFRESHES
OTHERS WILL HIM-
SELF BE REFRESHED.

PROVERBS 11:25 NIV

would endear him to others throughout his life. When Johannes left home at the age of fifteen to pursue a musical career, his mother remained a powerful influence in his life through the hundreds of letters she wrote to him.

Johannes' mother always saw the best in people and was confident in her son's abilities. When a famous violinist named Reményi once severed his connection with Brahms, she wrote, "I hope you have parted friends. After all one can't be angry with him. He probably thinks he is better off on his own . . . with you he may make a good impression at the moment, but not in the long run."

In fact, the only bitterness Christiane ever acknowledged was in not having the financial means to help others. "What can give me greater joy than to help and serve my fellow-creatures as far as lies in my power," she once wrote. "People who live only for themselves and not for others are only half alive."

Christiane implicitly trusted in God, and because of Johannes Brahms' depth of biblical understanding, it has been surmised that her influence over her son was spiritual as well as emotional and intellectual. Once when Johannes was attacked for his lack of interest in the organized church, he said, "Nevertheless, I do have my faith."

Johanna Christiane Brahms gave the world her son, Johannes, who in turn shared his remarkable gift of music, especially in his famous four symphonies, piano music, lullabies, and masterpieces such as *The German Requiem*.

A Mother of Influence nurtures communication with her children.

LIEUWKJE VAN DER BIJL

1890 - 1948

BROTHER ANDREW'S mother, who prayed unceasingly for her son, passed away before she saw his missionary work turn into a world organization that has smuggled millions of Bibles into closed countries all over the world.

❧

On Sunday mornings in a small village in Holland, Mrs. van der Bijl always gathered her neatly dressed, freshly scrubbed children together, and after Father locked the door, the family would set off for the Dutch Reform church. Once there, they would squeeze tightly into the pew, which never seemed to be long enough to hold all of them, giving her son Andrew an excuse to duck out the back door.

One morning, Mother noticed her husband, two daughters, and four sons sitting quietly in the row alongside her and then standing to sing the first hymn, but Andrew was missing. How had he managed to sneak away again? His mother couldn't understand why the subject of God and church made young Andrew so uncomfortable, but she prayed even more fervently for his eternal soul, as well as his life's work.

A prankster and daredevil as a child, Andrew once threw firecrackers at German soldiers occupying the streets of his hometown during World War II, and another time he poured sugar in the gas tank of a Nazi general's car to ruin the engine. His mother guessed what he had done and kept silent about the shortage of sugar in her pantry.

Andrew joined the army as a nineteen-year-old, looking for adventure, and in the East Indies he captured ten armed guerillas without any help from his commando unit. Andrew was so daring and fearless that he occasionally wore a yellow straw hat in combat, making himself an easy

[PAUL SAID,] "GOD KNOWS HOW OFTEN I PRAY FOR YOU. DAY AND NIGHT I BRING YOU AND YOUR NEEDS IN PRAYER TO GOD, WHOM I SERVE WITH ALL MY HEART BY TELLING OTHERS THE GOOD NEWS ABOUT HIS SON."

ROMANS 1:9 NLT

target for the enemy. He could have led the life of a self-indulgent rebel, but God intervened. Recuperating in the hospital after being wounded, Andrew read the Bible from cover to cover several times. "Brother Andrew," as he came to be known, dedicated his life to God.

Years later on a trip to Poland, he witnessed the emptiness of communism and learned there were few Bibles in the Soviet-bloc countries. Inspired by God he began to smuggle the Scriptures that had so radically changed his life to the people trapped in those spiritually starving communist nations.

Although he had avoided prayer as a boy, now that he was doing God's work, Brother Andrew made it a practice to utter a quick "smuggler's prayer" on his many dangerous border crossings into Iron Curtain countries. "Father, You have made blind eyes to see," he would pray. "Now I ask You to make seeing eyes blind."

Since those early days, Brother Andrew's solitary mission has turned into an international ministry, and millions of Bibles have been smuggled into places where Christianity is outlawed or severely restricted.

"I'm not brave," Brother Andrew has said, "I'm often scared stiff. I drive my car to the Iron Curtain border in the past and I have not the guts to go on. So I pull back ten miles, find a small hotel, I begin to pray and fast until I have the courage, or the liberty or the boldness to go in and that always works."

Andrew's mother would not live to see the fruit of her prayers for her son's life, but her example turned the boy who avoided church into a man after God's own heart.

A Mother of Influence prays for her children's futures.

HANNAH CHAMBERS

Unknown

OSWALD CHAMBERS' mother, Hannah, who had dedicated

her life to her husband and family as a pastor's wife, supported

her son as he followed in his father's footsteps.

❦

Hannah sat with her husband, Clarence, at their cozy kitchen table, enjoying afternoon tea, while outside fog draped over the thick branches of barren trees. She smiled as she placed her hand over her husband's and lovingly looked into his face framed by white hair. His eightieth birthday was only three weeks away.

Their silent moment was interrupted by the harsh intrusion of the doorbell. It rang a few times before their daughter-in-law Gertrude could answer the summons and receive a telegram from the person at the door. She returned to the warm kitchen with an envelope, which she promptly handed to her father, who opened it. Reading aloud, he said, "OSWALD IN HIS PRESENCE."

Stunned, those four words relayed the message that their forty-three-year-old son and husband was dead. The Chambers family had no details as to why or how, but they numbly began to write other family members and friends: ". . . Cable just received from Cairo . . . Oswald with the Lord . . . will send more as we know." How difficult for a mother to out-live her youngest son without even the chance to say good-bye!

Through her tears, Hannah remembered Oswald as a young man influenced by Charles H. Spurgeon, dedicating his life to the things of God, and then going on to study theology at Dunoon College. Only six years before his death, her son had founded the Bible Training College in Clapham, London, which was forced to close in 1915 due to World War I.

FOR TO ME, TO LIVE IS CHRIST, AND TO DIE IS GAIN.

PHILIPPIANS 1:21 NASB

He had set sail for Zeitoun, Egypt (near Cairo), later that same year as a YMCA chaplain for the troops stationed there. But just a month after his arrival in Egypt, his appendix ruptured, the family learned later, and he died shortly after surgery on November 15, 1917.

Even though he was gone, Hannah knew in her heart that her son still had a wonderful gift for the world. But it would be his wife, Gertrude "Bitty" Chambers (who had taken shorthand notes of all his lectures) who would spend the next fifty years compiling and helping to publish his work so that others might be touched and inspired by this man of God.

Oswald Chambers's classic devotional, *My Utmost for His Highest*, has been in print since 1935 in the United States, and today still ranks in the top ten titles of religious best-sellers.

A Mother of Influence supports her children's career choices.

MOTHERS *of* THE BIBLE

BATHSHEBA

Mother of Solomon

She would not allow King David to forget his

promise to her concerning her son.

⸺❦⸺

Bathsheba went into the king's bedroom. He was very old now, and Abishag was taking care of him. Bathsheba bowed low before him. "What can I do for you?" he asked her. She replied, "My lord, you vowed to me by the LORD your God that my son Solomon would be the next king and would sit on your throne."

1 KINGS 1:15-17 NLT

King David said, "Call in Bathsheba." So she came into the king's presence and stood before him. The king then took an oath: "As surely as the LORD lives, who has delivered me out of every trouble, I will surely carry out today what I swore to you by the LORD, the God of Israel: Solomon your son shall be king after me, and he will sit on my throne in my place." Then Bathsheba bowed low with her face to the ground and, kneeling before the king, said, "May my lord King David live forever!"

1 KINGS 1:28-31 NIV

Go forth, O daughters of Zion, and gaze on King Solomon with the crown with which his mother has crowned him on the day of his wedding, and on the day of his gladness of heart."

SONG OF SOLOMON 3:11 NASB

DEBORAH

Mother of Israel

When the leaders of Israel lacked courage and direction, she

stepped forward and lead them to victory.

Deborah, a prophetess, the wife of Lapidoth, was judging Israel at that time. And she would sit under the palm tree of Deborah between Ramah and Bethel in the mountains of Ephraim. And the children of Israel came up to her for judgment. Then she sent and called for Barak the son of Abinoam from Kedesh in Naphtali, and said to him, "Has not the LORD God of Israel commanded, 'Go and deploy troops at Mount Tabor; take with you ten thousand men of the sons of Naphtali and of the sons of Zebulun; and against you I will deploy Sisera, the commander of Jabin's army, with his chariots and his multitude at the River Kishon; and I will deliver him into your hand'?"

And Barak said to her, "If you will go with me, then I will go; but if you will not go with me, I will not go!"

So she said, "I will surely go with you; nevertheless there will be no glory for you in the journey you are taking, for the LORD will sell Sisera into the hand of a woman." Then Deborah arose and went with Barak to Kedesh. And Barak called Zebulun and Naphtali to Kedesh; he went up with ten thousand men under his command, and Deborah went up with him.

JUDGES 4:4-10 NKJV

The Song of Deborah

Deborah and Barak son of Abinoam sang on that day, saying:

"When locks are long in Israel,
when the people offer themselves willingly—
bless the LORD!

"Hear, O kings; give ear, O princes;
to the LORD I will sing,
I will make melody to the LORD, the God of Israel.

"LORD, when you went out from Seir,
when you marched from the region of Edom,
the earth trembled,
and the heavens poured,
the clouds indeed poured water.

"The mountains quaked before the LORD, the One of Sinai,
before the LORD, the God of Israel.

"In the days of Shamgar son of Anath,
in the days of Jael, caravans ceased
and travelers kept to the byways.

"The peasantry prospered in Israel,
they grew fat on plunder,
because you arose, Deborah,
arose as a mother in Israel.

"Awake, awake, Deborah!
Awake, awake, utter a song!
Arise, Barak, lead away your captives,
O son of Abinoam."

JUDGES 5:1-7, 12 NRSV

ELIZABETH

Mother of John the Baptist

She held onto the promise that her son would become the
forerunner of the Messiah, even though his lifestyle was maligned and
he was martyred at a young age.

∞

In the time of Herod king of Judea there was a priest named
Zechariah, who belonged to the priestly division of Abijah; his wife
Elizabeth was also a descendant of Aaron. Both of them were upright in
the sight of God, observing all the Lord's commandments and regulations
blamelessly. But they had no children, because Elizabeth was barren; and
they were both well along in years.

LUKE 1:5-7 NIV

The angel reassured him, "Don't fear, Zachariah. Your prayer has
been heard. Elizabeth, your wife, will bear a son by you. You are to name
him John. You're going to leap like a gazelle for joy, and not only you—
many will delight in his birth. He'll achieve great stature with God.

LUKE 1:13-15 MSG

Soon afterward his wife, Elizabeth, became pregnant and went into
seclusion for five months. "How kind the Lord is!" she exclaimed. "He
has taken away my disgrace of having no children!"

LUKE 1:24-25 NLT

"Behold, even your relative Elizabeth has also conceived a son in her
old age; and she who was called barren is now in her sixth month. For

nothing will be impossible with God." And Mary said, "Behold, the bond-slave of the Lord; be it done to me according to your word." And the angel departed from her.

LUKE 1:36-38 NASB

It happened, when Elizabeth heard the greeting of Mary that the babe leaped in her womb; and Elizabeth was filled with the Holy Spirit. Then she spoke out with a loud voice and said, "Blessed are you among women, and blessed is the fruit of your womb! But why is this granted to me, that the mother of my Lord should come to me? For indeed, as soon as the voice of your greeting sounded in my ears, the babe leaped in my womb for joy. Blessed is she who believed, for there will be a fulfillment of those things which were told her from the Lord."

LUKE 1:41-45 NKJV

Elisabeth's full time came that she should be delivered; and she brought forth a son. And her neighbours and her cousins heard how the Lord had shewed great mercy upon her; and they rejoiced with her.

LUKE 1:57- 58 KJV

You, my child, will be called a prophet of the Most High; for you will go on before the Lord to prepare the way for him, to give his people the knowledge of salvation through the forgiveness of their sins.

LUKE 1:76-77 NIV

ELISHA'S MOTHER

She gave her son to the Lord to serve as His prophet.

⤬

Elijah went straight out and found Elisha son of Shaphat in a field where there were twelve pairs of yoked oxen at work plowing; Elisha was in charge of the twelfth pair. Elijah went up to him and threw his cloak over him.

Elisha deserted the oxen, ran after Elijah, and said, "Please! Let me kiss my father and mother good-bye—then I'll follow you."

"Go ahead," said Elijah, "but, mind you, don't forget what I've just done to you."

So Elisha left; he took his yoke of oxen and butchered them. He made a fire with the plow and tackle and then boiled the meat—a true farewell meal for the family. Then he left and followed Elijah, becoming his right-hand man.

1 KINGS 19:19-21 MSG

EUNICE

Mother of Timothy

She passed along her genuine faith to her son, Timothy, who

became a leader in the early church.

❧✖✖❧

He [Paul] came to Derbe and then to Lystra, where a disciple named Timothy lived, whose mother was a Jewess and a believer, but whose father was a Greek.

ACTS 16:1 NIV

I am reminded of your sincere faith, a faith that lived first in your grandmother Lois and your mother Eunice and now, I am sure, lives in you. For this reason I remind you to rekindle the gift of God that is within you through the laying on of my hands; for God did not give us a spirit of cowardice, but rather a spirit of power and of love and of self-discipline.

2 TIMOTHY 1:5-7 NRSV

EVE

The First Mother

Even though she sinned against God, Eve showed her children—and all

those who could be born on earth in subsequent generations—the beauty

of repentance, forgiveness, and restoration.

⌇⋈⌇

[God said,] "And I will put enmity between you and the woman, and between your seed and her seed; he shall bruise you on the head, and you shall bruise him on the heel."

To the woman [God] said, "I will greatly multiply your pain in childbirth, in pain you shall bring forth children; yet your desire will be for your husband, and he will rule over you."

GENESIS 3:15-16 NASB

Adam called his wife's name Eve; because she was the mother of all living.

GENESIS 3:20 KJV

Adam lay with his wife Eve, and she became pregnant and gave birth to Cain. She said, "With the help of the LORD I have brought forth a man." Later she gave birth to his brother Abel. Now Abel kept flocks, and Cain worked the soil.

GENESIS 4:1-2 NIV

Adam slept with his wife again. She had a son whom she named Seth. She said, "God has given me another child in place of Abel whom Cain killed."

GENESIS 4:25 MSG

HAGAR

Mother of Ishmael

Mother of the Arab nations, she cried out to God for the life of her son,

and God heard and saved their lives.

⁓⚬❀⚬⁓

The angel of the LORD found her by a spring of water in the wilderness, the spring on the way to Shur. And he said, "Hagar, slave-girl of Sarai, where have you come from and where are you going?" She said, "I am running away from my mistress Sarai." The angel of the LORD said to her, "Return to your mistress, and submit to her." The angel of the LORD also said to her, "I will so greatly multiply your offspring that they cannot be counted for multitude." And the angel of the LORD said to her, "Now you have conceived and shall bear a son; you shall call him Ishmael, for the LORD has given heed to your affliction."

GENESIS 16:7-11 NRSV

[Hagar] went and sat down by herself about a hundred yards away. "I don't want to watch the boy die," she said, as she burst into tears.

Then God heard the boy's cries, and the angel of God called to Hagar from the sky, "Hagar, what's wrong? Do not be afraid! God has heard the boy's cries from the place where you laid him. Go to him and comfort him, for I will make a great nation from his descendants."

Then God opened Hagar's eyes, and she saw a well. She immediately filled her water container and gave the boy a drink.

GENESIS 21:16-19 NLT

HANNAH

Mother of Samuel

She promised her son to God's service, and when he was old enough,

she took him to the priest herself. Samuel became one of

the greatest prophets in Israel.

In bitterness of soul Hannah wept much and prayed to the LORD. And she made a vow, saying, "O LORD Almighty, if you will only look upon your servant's misery and remember me, and not forget your servant but give her a son, then I will give him to the LORD for all the days of his life, and no razor will ever be used on his head."

1 SAMUEL 1:10-11 NIV

It came about in due time, after Hannah had conceived, that she gave birth to a son; and she named him Samuel, saying, "Because I have asked him of the LORD."

1 SAMUEL 1:20 NASB

For this child I prayed; and the LORD hath given me my petition which I asked of him: Therefore also I have lent him to the LORD; as long as he liveth he shall be lent to the LORD. And he worshipped the LORD there.

1 SAMUEL 1:27-28 KJV

Hannah prayed:
I'm bursting with God-news! I'm walking on air. I'm laughing at my rivals. I'm dancing my salvation.
Nothing and no one is holy like GOD, no rock mountain like our

GOD.

Don't dare talk pretentiously—not a word of boasting, ever! For GOD knows what's going on. He takes the measure of everything that happens.

The weapons of the strong are smashed to pieces, while the weak are infused with fresh strength.

The well-fed are out begging in the streets for crusts, while the hungry are getting second helpings. The barren woman has a houseful of children, while the mother of many is bereft.

GOD brings death and GOD brings life, brings down to the grave and raises up.

GOD brings poverty and GOD brings wealth; he lowers, he also lifts up.

He puts poor people on their feet again; he rekindles burned-out lives with fresh hope, restoring dignity and respect to their lives—a place in the sun! For the very structures of earth are GOD'S; he has laid out his operations on a firm foundation.

He protectively cares for his faithful friends, step by step, but leaves the wicked to stumble in the dark. No one makes it in this life by sheer muscle!

GOD'S enemies will be blasted out of the sky, crashed in a heap and burned. GOD will set things right all over the earth, he'll give strength to his king, he'll set his anointed on top of the world!

1 SAMUEL 2:1-10 MSG

The LORD was gracious to Hannah; she conceived and gave birth to three sons and two daughters.

1 SAMUEL 2:21 NIV

JEDIDAH

Mother of King Josiah

She taught her son to do what was right

in the eyes of God.

⌐∞⌐

Josiah was eight years old when he became king, and he reigned in Jerusalem thirty-one years. His mother was Jedidah, the daughter of Adaiah from Bozkath. He did what was pleasing in the LORD'S sight and followed the example of his ancestor David. He did not turn aside from doing what was right.

2 KINGS 22:1- 2 NLT

Before him there was no king like him who turned to the LORD with all his heart and with all his soul and with all his might, according to all the law of Moses; nor did any like him arise after him.

2 KINGS 23:25 NASB

JOCHEBED

Mother of Moses, Aaron, and Miriam

She protected her children, believing that God had

a purpose for their lives.

⌙❦⌙

A man of the house of Levi married a Levite woman, and she became pregnant and gave birth to a son. When she saw that he was a fine child, she hid him for three months. But when she could hide him no longer, she got a papyrus basket for him and coated it with tar and pitch. Then she placed the child in it and put it among the reeds along the bank of the Nile. His sister stood at a distance to see what would happen to him.

EXODUS 2:1-4 NIV

Amram married his father's sister Jochebed, and she bore him Aaron and Moses. (Amram lived to be 137 years old.)

EXODUS 6:20 NLT

The name of Amram's wife was Jochebed the daughter of Levi, who was born to Levi in Egypt; and to Amram she bore Aaron and Moses and their sister Miriam.

NUMBERS 26:59 NKJV

LEAH

Mother of the Tribes of Israel

She prayed for God to open her womb, and He answered.

⌀

When GOD realized that Leah was unloved, he opened her womb. But Rachel was barren. Leah became pregnant and had a son. She named him Reuben (Look-It's-a-Boy!). "This is a sign," she said, "that GOD has seen my misery; and a sign that now my husband will love me."

She became pregnant again and had another son. "GOD heard," she said, "that I was unloved and so he gave me this son also." She named this one Simeon (GOD-Heard). She became pregnant yet again—another son. She said, "Now maybe my husband will connect with me—I've given him three sons!" That's why she named him Levi (Connect). She became pregnant a final time and had a fourth son. She said, "This time I'll praise God." So she named him Judah (Praise-God). Then she stopped having children.

GENESIS 29:31-35 MSG

Leah conceived again and bore Jacob a sixth son. Then Leah said, "God has presented me with a precious gift. This time my husband will treat me with honor, because I have borne him six sons." So she named him Zebulun.

GENESIS 30:19-21 NIV

MARY

Mother of Jesus

She called herself the "handmaiden" of the Lord.

In the sixth month the angel Gabriel was sent by God to a town in Galilee called Nazareth, to a virgin engaged to a man whose name was Joseph, of the house of David. The virgin's name was Mary. And he came to her and said, "Greetings, favored one! The Lord is with you." But she was much perplexed by his words and pondered what sort of greeting this might be. The angel said to her, "Do not be afraid, Mary, for you have found favor with God. And now, you will conceive in your womb and bear a son, and you will name him Jesus. He will be great, and will be called the Son of the Most High, and the Lord God will give to him the throne of his ancestor David. He will reign over the house of Jacob forever, and of his kingdom there will be no end."

LUKE 1:26-33 NRSV

It came to pass, that, when Elisabeth heard the salutation of Mary, the babe leaped in her womb; and Elisabeth was filled with the Holy Ghost: And she spake out with a loud voice, and said, Blessed art thou among women, and blessed is the fruit of thy womb.

LUKE 1:41-42 KJV

The Magnificat: Mary's Song of Praise

Mary responded, "Oh, how I praise the Lord
How I rejoice in God my Savior!
For he took notice of his lowly servant girl,
and now generation after generation
will call me blessed.
For he, the Mighty One, is holy,

and he has done great things for me.
His mercy goes on from generation to generation,
to all who fear him.
His mighty arm does tremendous things!
How he scatters the proud and haughty ones!
He has taken princes from their thrones
and exalted the lowly.
He has satisfied the hungry with good things
and sent the rich away with empty hands.
And how he has helped his servant Israel!
He has not forgotten his promise to be merciful.
For he promised our ancestors — Abraham and his children —
to be merciful to them forever."

LUKE 1:46-55 NLT

On the third day there was a wedding in Cana of Galilee, and the mother of Jesus was there. Now both Jesus and His disciples were invited to the wedding. And when they ran out of wine, the mother of Jesus said to Him, "They have no wine."

Jesus said to her, "Woman, what does your concern have to do with Me? My hour has not yet come."

His mother said to the servants, "Whatever He says to you, do it."

JOHN 2:1-5 NKJV

Jesus' mother, his aunt, Mary the wife of Clopas, and Mary Magdalene stood at the foot of the cross. Jesus saw his mother and the disciple he loved standing near her. He said to his mother, "Woman, here is your son." Then to the disciple, "Here is your mother." From that moment the disciple accepted her as his own mother.

JOHN 19:25-27 MSG

They all joined together constantly in prayer, along with the women and Mary the mother of Jesus, and with his brothers.

ACTS 1:14 NIV

MARY

Mother of James and John

She not only encouraged her sons to follow Jesus,

she did so herself.

❦

Many women were there looking on from a distance, who had followed Jesus from Galilee while ministering to Him. Among them was Mary Magdalene, and Mary the mother of James and Joseph, and the mother of the sons of Zebedee.

MATTHEW 27:55- 56 NASB

Mary Magdalene and the other Mary were there, sitting opposite the tomb.

MATTHEW 27:61 NRSV

Early on Sunday morning, as the new day was dawning, Mary Magdalene and the other Mary went out to see the tomb. Suddenly there was a great earthquake, because an angel of the Lord came down from heaven and rolled aside the stone and sat on it. His face shone like lightning, and his clothing was as white as snow. The guards shook with fear when they saw him, and they fell into a dead faint.

Then the angel spoke to the women. "Don't be afraid!" he said. "I know you are looking for Jesus, who was crucified. He isn't here! He has been raised from the dead, just as he said would happen. Come, see where his body was lying. And now, go quickly and tell his disciples he has been raised from the dead, and he is going ahead of you to Galilee. You will see him there. Remember, I have told you."

The women ran quickly from the tomb. They were very frightened but also filled with great joy, and they rushed to find the disciples to give them the angel's message. And as they went, Jesus met them. "Greetings!" he said. And they ran to him, held his feet, and worshiped him. Then Jesus said to them, "Don't be afraid! Go tell my brothers to leave for Galilee, and they will see me there."

MATTHEW 28:1-10 NLT

MOTHER OF BLIND SON

She spoke up for Jesus after he healed her son.

⟡

As Jesus was walking along, he saw a man who had been blind from birth. "Teacher," his disciples asked him, "why was this man born blind? Was it a result of his own sins or those of his parents?"

"It was not because of his sins or his parents' sins," Jesus answered. "He was born blind so the power of God could be seen in him.

JOHN 9:1-3 NLT

They asked them, "Is this your son? Was he born blind? If so, how can he see?"

His parents replied, "We know this is our son and that he was born blind, but we don't know how he can see or who healed him. He is old enough to speak for himself. Ask him." They said this because they were afraid of the Jewish leaders, who had announced that anyone saying Jesus was the Messiah would be expelled from the synagogue. That's why they said, "He is old enough to speak for himself. Ask him."

So for the second time they called in the man who had been blind and told him, "Give glory to God by telling the truth, because we know Jesus is a sinner."

"I don't know whether he is a sinner," the man replied. "But I know this: I was blind, and now I can see!"

JOHN 9:18-25 NLT

MOTHER IN KING SOLOMON'S COURT

She showed a mother's love by stepping aside to protect

the life of her child.

c∞ɔ

The king said, "Divide the living boy in two; then give half to the one, and half to the other." But the woman whose son was alive said to the king—because compassion for her son burned within her—"Please, my lord, give her the living boy; certainly do not kill him!" The other said, "It shall be neither mine nor yours; divide it." Then the king responded: "Give the first woman the living boy; do not kill him. She is his mother." All Israel heard of the judgment that the king had rendered; and they stood in awe of the king, because they perceived that the wisdom of God was in him, to execute justice.

1 KINGS 3:25-28 NRSV

MOTHER OF ZEBEDEE'S SONS

She asked Jesus to give her sons prominent places

in the kingdom of God.

❧

The mother of the sons of Zebedee came to Jesus with her sons, bowing down and making a request of Him. And He said to her, "What do you wish?" She said to Him, "Command that in Your kingdom these two sons of mine may sit one on Your right and one on Your left." But Jesus answered, "You do not know what you are asking. Are you able to drink the cup that I am about to drink?" They said to Him, "We are able." He said to them, "My cup you shall drink; but to sit on My right and on My left, this is not Mine to give, but it is for those for whom it has been prepared by My Father."

MATTHEW 20:20-23 NASB

Many women who followed Jesus from Galilee, ministering to Him, were there looking on from afar, among whom were Mary Magdalene, Mary the mother of James and Joses, and the mother of Zebedee's sons.

MATTHEW 27:55-56 NKJV

NAIN'S WIDOW

Her grief was so great that Jesus raised

her son from the dead.

❧

Soon afterward, Jesus went to a town called Nain, and his disciples and a large crowd went along with him. As he approached the town gate, a dead person was being carried out—the only son of his mother, and she was a widow. And a large crowd from the town was with her. When the Lord saw her, his heart went out to her and he said, "Don't cry."

Then he went up and touched the coffin, and those carrying it stood still. He said, "Young man, I say to you, get up!" The dead man sat up and began to talk, and Jesus gave him back to his mother.

LUKE 7:11-15 NIV

NAOMI

Mother-in-Law of Ruth

She taught her daughter-in-law Ruth that

the God of Israel is a God of love.

⌒∞⌒

After a short while on the road, Naomi told her two daughters-in-law, "Go back. Go home and live with your mothers. And may God treat you as graciously as you treated your deceased husbands and me. May God give each of you a new home and a new husband!" She kissed them and they cried openly.

RUTH 1:8-9 MSG

Again they wept together, and Orpah kissed her mother-in-law good-bye. But Ruth insisted on staying with Naomi. "See," Naomi said to her, "your sister-in-law has gone back to her people and to her gods. You should do the same."

But Ruth replied, "Don't ask me to leave you and turn back. I will go wherever you go and live wherever you live. Your people will be my people, and your God will be my God. I will die where you die and will be buried there. May the LORD punish me severely if I allow anything but death to separate us!" So when Naomi saw that Ruth had made up her mind to go with her, she stopped urging her.

RUTH 1:14-18 NLT

Boaz married Ruth and took her home to live with him. When he slept with her, the LORD enabled her to become pregnant, and she gave birth to a son. And the women of the town said to Naomi, "Praise the LORD who has given you a family redeemer today! May he be famous in

Israel. May this child restore your youth and care for you in your old age. For he is the son of your daughter-in-law who loves you so much and who has been better to you than seven sons!"

Naomi took care of the baby and cared for him as if he were her own. The neighbor women said, "Now at last Naomi has a son again!" And they named him Obed. He became the father of Jesse and the grandfather of David.

RUTH 4:13-17NLT

PHARAOH'S DAUGHTER

Foster Mother of Moses

She reached out to an infant, helpless and condemned,

and gave him a future.

Pharaoh's daughter went down to the Nile to bathe, and her attendants were walking along the river bank. She saw the basket among the reeds and sent her slave girl to get it. She opened it and saw the baby. He was crying, and she felt sorry for him. "This is one of the Hebrew babies," she said.

Then his sister asked Pharaoh's daughter, "Shall I go and get one of the Hebrew women to nurse the baby for you?"

"Yes, go," she answered. And the girl went and got the baby's mother. Pharaoh's daughter said to her, "Take this baby and nurse him for me, and I will pay you." So the woman took the baby and nursed him. When the child grew older, she took him to Pharaoh's daughter and he became her son. She named him Moses, saying, "I drew him out of the water."

EXODUS 2:5-10 NIV

RACHEL

Mother of Joseph

She gave her life for her children.

∾⪻∾

When Rachel saw that she bore Jacob no children, she became jealous of her sister; and she said to Jacob, "Give me children, or else I die." Then Jacob's anger burned against Rachel, and he said, "Am I in the place of God, who has withheld from you the fruit of the womb?"

GENESIS 30:1-2 NASB

God remembered Rachel, and God heeded her and opened her womb. She conceived and bore a son, and said, "God has taken away my reproach"; and she named him Joseph, saying, "May the LORD add to me another son!"

GENESIS 30:22-24 NKJV

GENESIS 30:22-24 NRSV

REBEKAH

Mother of Jacob and Esau

She left the life she knew to become a wife and mother.

They said, "We will call the young woman and ask her personally."
Then they called Rebekah and said to her, "Will you go with this man?"
And she said, "I will go."
So they sent away Rebekah their sister and her nurse, and Abraham's
servant and his men. And they blessed Rebekah and said to her:
"Our sister, may you become
The mother of thousands of ten thousands;
And may your descendants possess
The gates of those who hate them."

GENESIS 24:57-60 NKJV

Isaac sent away Jacob: and he went to Padan-aram unto Laban, son
of Bethuel the Syrian, the brother of Rebekah, Jacob's and Esau's mother.

GENESIS 28:5 KJV

RUTH

Mother of Obed

Her son became an ancestor of Jesus Christ.

⚬⧢⚬

Boaz announced to the elders and all the people, "Today you are witnesses that I have bought from Naomi all the property of Elimelech, Kilion and Mahlon. I have also acquired Ruth the Moabitess, Mahlon's widow, as my wife, in order to maintain the name of the dead with his property, so that his name will not disappear from among his family or from the town records. Today you are witnesses!"

So Boaz took Ruth and she became his wife. Then he went to her, and the LORD enabled her to conceive, and she gave birth to a son. The women said to Naomi: "Praise be to the LORD, who this day has not left you without a kinsman-redeemer. May he become famous throughout Israel! He will renew your life and sustain you in your old age. For your daughter-in-law, who loves you and who is better to you than seven sons, has given him birth."

Then Naomi took the child, laid him in her lap and cared for him. The women living there said, "Naomi has a son." And they named him Obed. He was the father of Jesse, the father of David.

RUTH 4:9-10; 13-17 NIV

SAMSON'S MOTHER

She raised her son according to the instructions

given to her by God.

❦

The woman went to her husband and said, "A man of God came to me. He looked like the angel of God—terror laced with glory! I didn't ask him where he was from and he didn't tell me his name, but he told me, 'You're pregnant. You're going to give birth to a son. Don't drink any wine or beer and eat nothing ritually unclean. The boy will be God's Nazirite from the moment of birth to the day of his death.'

Manoah prayed to God: "Master, let the man of God you sent come to us again and teach us how to raise this boy who is to be born."

JUDGES 13:6-8 MSG

The angel of the LORD replied, "Be sure your wife follows the instructions I gave her. She must not eat grapes or raisins, drink wine or any other alcoholic drink, or eat any forbidden food."

Then Manoah said to the angel of the LORD, "Please stay here until we can prepare a young goat for you to eat."

JUDGES 13:13-15 NLT

The woman bore a son and called his name Samson; and the child grew, and the LORD blessed him.

JUDGES 13:24 NKJV

SARAH

Mother of Isaac

She gave birth in her old age to a son,

God's servant.

∂⧸⧹∂

God said to Abraham, "As for Sarai your wife, you shall not call her name Sarai, but Sarah shall be her name. I will bless her, and indeed I will give you a son by her. Then I will bless her, and she shall be a mother of nations; kings of peoples will come from her." Then Abraham fell on his face and laughed, and said in his heart, "Will a child be born to a man one hundred years old? And will Sarah, who is ninety years old, bear a child?" And Abraham said to God, "Oh that Ishmael might live before You!" But God said, "No, but Sarah your wife shall bear you a son, and you shall call his name Isaac; and I will establish My covenant with him for an everlasting covenant for his descendants after him."

GENESIS 17:15-19 NASB

They said to him, "Where is your wife Sarah?" And he said, "There, in the tent." Then one said, "I will surely return to you in due season, and your wife Sarah shall have a son." And Sarah was listening at the tent entrance behind him. Now Abraham and Sarah were old, advanced in age; it had ceased to be with Sarah after the manner of women. So Sarah laughed to herself, saying, "After I have grown old, and my husband is old, shall I have pleasure?" The LORD said to Abraham, "Why did Sarah laugh, and say, 'Shall I indeed bear a child, now that I am old?' Is anything too wonderful for the LORD? At the set time I will return to you, in due season, and Sarah shall have a son."

GENESIS 18:9-14 NRSV

The Lord visited Sarah as He had said, and the Lord did for Sarah as He had spoken. For Sarah conceived and bore Abraham a son in his old age, at the set time of which God had spoken to him. And Abraham called the name of his son who was born to him-whom Sarah bore to him-Isaac.

GENESIS 21:1-3 NKJV

SHUNAMMITE MOTHER

She beseeched the prophet Elisha to ask God

to give her a son.

⁓∞⁓

One day Elisha went to the town of Shunem. A wealthy woman lived there, and she invited him to eat some food. From then on, whenever he passed that way, he would stop there to eat.

She said to her husband, "I am sure this man who stops in from time to time is a holy man of God. Let's make a little room for him on the roof and furnish it with a bed, a table, a chair, and a lamp. Then he will have a place to stay whenever he comes by."

One day Elisha returned to Shunem, and he went up to his room to rest. He said to his servant Gehazi, "Tell the woman I want to speak to her." When she arrived, Elisha said to Gehazi, "Tell her that we appreciate the kind concern she has shown us. Now ask her what we can do for her. Does she want me to put in a good word for her to the king or to the commander of the army?"

"No," she replied, "my family takes good care of me."

Later Elisha asked Gehazi, "What do you think we can do for her?"

He suggested, "She doesn't have a son, and her husband is an old man."

"Call her back again," Elisha told him. When the woman returned, Elisha said to her as she stood in the doorway, "Next year at about this time you will be holding a son in your arms!"

"No, my lord!" she protested. "Please don't lie to me like that, O man of God." But sure enough, the woman soon became pregnant. And at that time the following year she had a son, just as Elisha had said.

2 KINGS 4:8-17 NLT

The child grew up. One day he went to his father, who was working with the harvest hands, complaining, "My head, my head!"

His father ordered a servant, "Carry him to his mother."

The servant took him in his arms and carried him to his mother. He lay on her lap until noon and died.

She took him up and laid him on the bed of the man of God, shut him in alone, and left.

2 KINGS 4:18-21 MSG

The mother of the lad said, "As the LORD lives and as you yourself live, I will not leave you." And he arose and followed her. Then Gehazi passed on before them and laid the staff on the lad's face, but there was no sound or response. So he returned to meet him and told him, "The lad has not awakened." When Elisha came into the house, behold the lad was dead and laid on his bed. So he entered and shut the door behind them both, and prayed to the LORD.

2 KINGS 4:30-33 NASB

Elisha summoned Gehazi and said, "Call the Shunammite woman." So he called her. When she came to him, he said, "Take your son." She came and fell at his feet, bowing to the ground; then she took her son and left.

2 KINGS 4:36-37 NRSV

SYRO-PHOENICIAN MOTHER

Her faith convinced Jesus to heal her child.

⌒⊗⌒

A Canaanite woman from that vicinity came to him, crying out, "Lord, Son of David, have mercy on me! My daughter is suffering terribly from demon-possession."

Jesus did not answer a word. So his disciples came to him and urged him, "Send her away, for she keeps crying out after us."

He answered, "I was sent only to the lost sheep of Israel."

The woman came and knelt before him. "Lord, help me!" she said.

He replied, "It is not right to take the children's bread and toss it to their dogs."

"Yes, Lord," she said, "but even the dogs eat the crumbs that fall from their masters' table."

Then Jesus answered, "Woman, you have great faith! Your request is granted." And her daughter was healed from that very hour.

MATTHEW 15:22-28 NIV

Widow with Two Sons

She followed the instructions of the prophet Elisha and

saved the lives of her sons.

⸎

One day the widow of one of Elisha's fellow prophets came to Elisha and cried out to him, "My husband who served you is dead, and you know how he feared the LORD. But now a creditor has come, threatening to take my two sons as slaves."

"What can I do to help you?" Elisha asked. "Tell me, what do you have in the house?"

"Nothing at all, except a flask of olive oil," she replied.

And Elisha said, "Borrow as many empty jars as you can from your friends and neighbors. Then go into your house with your sons and shut the door behind you. Pour olive oil from your flask into the jars, setting the jars aside as they are filled."

So she did as she was told. Her sons brought many jars to her, and she filled one after another. Soon every container was full to the brim!

"Bring me another jar," she said to one of her sons.

"There aren't any more!" he told her. And then the olive oil stopped flowing.

When she told the man of God what had happened, he said to her, "Now sell the olive oil and pay your debts, and there will be enough money left over to support you and your sons."

2 KINGS 4:1-7 NLT

ZAREPHATH WIDOW

She served the prophet Elijah and asked him to

raise her son from the dead.

⌒∽⌖∽

[The Lord said to Elijah,] "Arise, go to Zarephath, which belongs to Sidon, and stay there; behold, I have commanded a widow there to provide for you."

1 KINGS 17:9 NASB

[Elijah] went to Zarephath. As he arrived at the gates of the village, he saw a widow gathering sticks, and he asked her, "Would you please bring me a cup of water?" As she was going to get it, he called to her, "Bring me a bite of bread, too."

But she said, "I swear by the LORD your God that I don't have a single piece of bread in the house. And I have only a handful of flour left in the jar and a little cooking oil in the bottom of the jug. I was just gathering a few sticks to cook this last meal, and then my son and I will die."

But Elijah said to her, "Don't be afraid! Go ahead and cook that 'last meal,' but bake me a little loaf of bread first. Afterward there will still be enough food for you and your son. For this is what the LORD, the God of Israel, says: There will always be plenty of flour and oil left in your containers until the time when the LORD sends rain and the crops grow again!"

So she did as Elijah said, and she and Elijah and her son continued to eat from her supply of flour and oil for many days. For no matter how much they used, there was always enough left in the containers, just as the LORD had promised through Elijah.

Some time later, the woman's son became sick. He grew worse and worse, and finally he died. She then said to Elijah, "O man of God, what have you done to me? Have you come here to punish my sins by killing my son?"

But Elijah replied, "Give me your son." And he took the boy's body from her, carried him up to the upper room, where he lived, and laid the body on his bed. Then Elijah cried out to the LORD, "O LORD my God, why have you brought tragedy on this widow who has opened her home to me, causing her son to die?"

And he stretched himself out over the child three times and cried out to the LORD, "O LORD my God, please let this child's life return to him." The LORD heard Elijah's prayer, and the life of the child returned, and he came back to life! Then Elijah brought him down from the upper room and gave him to his mother. "Look, your son is alive!" he said.

Then the woman told Elijah, "Now I know for sure that you are a man of God, and that the LORD truly speaks through you."

1 KINGS 17:10-24 NLT

THE PROVERBS 31 MOTHER

A Woman of Noble Character

❦

Although Proverbs 31 was written for a Jewish audience, Christians have long used it as an example for godly women. Traditionally, Jewish men and women would recite this proverb on Friday night of the Sabbath as the family gathered around the table.

Like the old adage that says "beauty is as beauty does," according to Proverbs 31, the value of a woman does not depend on her physical beauty, but rather on her inner qualities, which are manifested in charitable actions toward her family and community.

The aristocratic woman described in Proverbs 31 seems to be a supermother, making it almost impossible for anyone to live up to all her ideals. She runs a household full of servants, owns real estate and manages a vineyard, is a shrewd businesswoman, and keeps the household running smoothly, while also performing acts of charity. Some Bible scholars believe the Proverbs 31 woman is a symbol of wisdom, which has merit since the entire book of Proverbs is intended as wisdom literature.

Whether taken literally or symbolically, the Proverbs 31 mother has inspired women for generations to live in fear of the Lord and to be faithful to their families and communities, giving their gifts, talents, and time to the service of others. Doing so promises that her children will "respect and bless her," and her husband will join in with "words of praise."

A good woman is hard to find,
and worth far more than diamonds.

Her husband trusts her without reserve,
and never has reason to regret it.

Never spiteful, she treats him generously
all her life long.

She shops around for the best yarns and cottons,
and enjoys knitting and sewing.

She's like a trading ship that sails to faraway places
and brings back exotic surprises.

She's up before dawn, preparing breakfast
for her family and organizing her day.

She looks over a field and buys it,
then, with money she's put aside, plants a garden.

First thing in the morning, she dresses for work,
rolls up her sleeves, eager to get started.

She senses the worth of her work,
is in no hurry to call it quits for the day.

She's skilled in the crafts of home and hearth,
diligent in homemaking.

She's quick to assist anyone in need,
reaches out to help the poor.

She doesn't worry about her family when it snows;
their winter clothes are all mended and ready to wear.

She makes her own clothing,
and dresses in colorful linens and silks.

Her husband is greatly respected
when he deliberates with the city fathers.

She designs gowns and sells them,
brings the sweaters she knits to the dress shops.

Her clothes are well-made and elegant,
and she always faces tomorrow with a smile.

When she speaks she has something worthwhile to say,
and she always says it kindly.

She keeps an eye on everyone in her household,
and keeps them all busy and productive.

Her children respect and bless her;
her husband joins in with words of praise:

"Many women have done wonderful things,
but you've outclassed them all!"

Charm can mislead and beauty soon fades.
The woman to be admired and praised
is the woman who lives in the Fear-of-GOD.

Give her everything she deserves!
Festoon her life with praises!

PROVERBS 31:10-31 MSG

PRAYERS *for* YOUR CHILDREN

PRAYING FOR SMALL CHILDREN

TRAIN A CHILD HOW TO LIVE THE RIGHT WAY. THEN EVEN
WHEN HE IS OLD, HE WILL STILL LIVE THAT WAY.
PROVERBS 22:6 NCV

TEACH THEM THE STATUTES AND THE LAWS, AND MAKE
KNOWN TO THEM THE WAY IN WHICH THEY ARE TO WALK,
AND THE WORK THEY ARE TO DO.
EXODUS 18:20 NASB

YOU SHALL FEED YOUR FLOCK LIKE A SHEPHERD: YOU
SHALL GATHER WITH YOUR ARM, AND CARRY THEM CLOSE
TO YOUR CHEST, AND SHALL GENTLY LEAD THOSE, LIKE ME,
WHO ARE WITH YOUNG.
ISAIAH 40:11 PERSONALIZED

Heavenly Father,

Raising small children is a task unlike any other I have faced. It is all
hands on deck, 24/7, with very few breaks. There are few *thank-yous*, little
appreciation for the self-sacrifice the assignment requires. And yet, sometimes it's the most rewarding job on earth.

I'm thankful that You gently lead me during this season of my life. I put
even more demands on myself than You put on me. Help me to relax a bit
and to keep my priorities straight. A spotless house is not that important
when my children need my full attention. Help me to turn a blind eye to
the dust that stands in all the corners.

I know it won't always be this difficult, although new challenges will
arise. Help me to enjoy the special moments today, each one of them a
seed for a precious memory. Give me strength and enable me to be the
mother my little children need. Amen.

Praying for Teens

Wise Father,

Jesus was a teen once, so You must know what I am going through. So much vitality and optimism; they think they can conquer the world. Other days, raging hormones push them to the other end of the spectrum, driving me to prayer on my knees!

Thank You for the precious teens You have given me. The thrill of youth brings our home to life when they walk through the door. It reminds me of my own youth, such an exciting time of life.

But my teens are no longer small children, and I have to adapt to this new level in parenting. If I hover over them too much, they are sure to draw back. But if I give them too much freedom, they are likely to get hurt. Lord, I need You to show me the middle ground. Give me the wisdom to know where I can ease up their restrictions, but keep me sensitive, so I will know when they need me to step in. Amen.

PRAYING FOR ADULT CHILDREN

SHOW RESPECT FOR EVERYONE.
1 PETER 2:17 TLB

DO NOT NAG YOUR CHILDREN. IF YOU ARE TOO HARD TO PLEASE, THEY MAY WANT TO STOP TRYING.
COLOSSIANS 3:21 NCV

I PRAYED FOR THIS CHILD, AND THE LORD HAS GRANTED ME WHAT I ASKED OF HIM. SO NOW I GIVE HIM TO THE LORD. FOR HIS WHOLE LIFE HE WILL BE GIVEN OVER TO THE LORD.
1 SAMUEL 1:27-28 NIV

WITH ALL HUMILITY AND GENTLENESS, WITH PATIENCE, I AM TO FORBEAR OTHERS IN LOVE.
EPHESIANS 4:2 PERSONALIZED

Heavenly Father,

When I gave birth to my children, it was hard to imagine they would ever become adults; yet the time has come, and they are no longer living under my roof. Although I'm still their mother, my role has changed and I need Your help.

It is no longer my job to tell them what they should do. I had eighteen years to invest my values in them, but now they must stand on their own. I pray You will help them and catch them if they fall. At those times when I don't approve, help me to show them the respect they deserve. Whenever possible, I will be quick to extend my blessing.

Help me to keep my tongue and not offer unsolicited advice. Should they marry, help me to accept their spouses as wonderful additions to our family. And if they have children, help me to be the support they need without interfering.

Thank You for helping me adapt. Amen.

Index by Child's Name

Children of
Mothers of the Bible